BIRTH OF A

CHRISTIAN ANARCHIST

by

George Tarleton

PENDRAGON PRESS
PENNINGTON

A PENDRAGON PRESS Book

First published in Great Britain in 1993 by
Pendragon Press Pennington

British Library Cataloguing-in-Publication Data
A catalogue record for this book is available
from the British Library

ISBN 1 874746 04 4

This book was designed and typeset by
Pendragon Press Pennington
Lymington SO41 8DX
Printed by Hobbs the Printers Limited, Southampton

MENE MENE TEKEL U-PHARSIN

This book is dedicated to those
who have tried Christianity
and found it wanting

ACKNOWLEDGEMENTS

My thanks to all those mentioned in this book as you helped to shape my life and point me — sometimes unwittingly — in the direction of my new-found freedom. In particular, I would like to single out the following people:

Professor Elaine Pagles who, through *'The Gnostic Gospels'* gave me a revolutionary insight into the complex origins of Christianity.

Doctor Andrew Walker who initially encouraged me to write this book, even though he does not share my anarchic perspective.

Laurie Young for his blunt, detailed criticism which forced me to re-write the whole book — only a real friend can be that honest.

Dorothy Tarleton for living the book with me and becoming a wonderfully independent woman as a result of the experience.

CONTENTS

Appendices

INTRODUCTION

We are all seekers, finders and seekers still. Searching for truth has dominated my adult life. Once I was so convinced I had found it, I preached it to thousands. Now I am in the hunt again and it's exciting. So what is truth? Ironically, this question is raised in the oldest fragment we have of the New Testament. This scrap of parchment contains just a couple of verses, one of them has Pilate's searching question in it.

To me, truth is a strong, beautiful woman. Because she is always immaculately dressed in the latest facts, many look no further. How sad to imagine you have discovered the truth by merely unearthing cold, hard facts. Facts need to be evaluated. Lawyers manipulate them. Politicians play with them. Truth lies beyond the fabric of facts.

Once you get beneath her dress you find her cultural underwear. Each culture readily accepts certain things, while rejecting whatever does not fit in with their cosy customs. No matter how seductive, we need to go beyond this homespun chastity belt. When you get to see the naked truth, you can simply remain an observer. It's called the scientific approach. No one can blame you for remaining a voyeur, for truth in all her naked splendour is truly magnificent.

However, some new physicists are beginning to see that we cannot be that objective. What we see as physical reality, they say, is merely our interpretation of it. Reality is what each of us decides it is. The word Pilate used for 'truth' means not only a knowledge of what is true, but also an experience of what is real. Truth is a warm, living body which we can experience. Books can only take you so far.

The holy books of all the world's religions are like different parts of a sex manual. Because the founder of their religion encountered truth in a certain position, the followers claim it is the only way. Fundamentalists always seem to opt for the missionary position. You can try all the different techniques and still end up with just a momentary thrill. The secret is learning to ride the wave of ecstasy.

Truth responds to love. She must be given time to reveal her secrets, not raped. Knowing truth involves intimacy: Adam knew Eve and she conceived. For too long we have separated knowing from being. When you know something in the depth of your being it sets you free. Free to be. Free to become. Free to beget. A love affair with the truth always produces something divinely human. The Word is made flesh. Whatever is born is unique to you. This book contains what is unique to me.

BURMESE DAZE

The noise was ear-splitting. Bombs seemed to be exploding everywhere followed by the dull thud of metal entering human flesh. Flames shot up into the sky. People started screaming and only then did I become aware of the bright red blood. Now people were running in all directions. Women were crying and so was I. My mother stoically grabbed my hand and dragged me through this nightmare. But I did not wake up. This was no bad dream. It was the first thing I remember as a child.

War had broken out. How do you explain that to a four-year old boy? Dad had gone to India to join the British Army. They promised him we would be flown out to join him but the last plane had left. Stranded in Burma, my mother and grandparents made a hasty decision. We would trek north east to the relative safety of India.

The Japanese landed in Burma just before Christmas 1941. Within two months they had driven the British out of Rangoon, the capital of Burma. Forced to retreat, the troops were compelled to withdraw to India. Hot on their heels the Japanese burned every major town to the ground, cutting off any escape route. All I remember is a village being bombed and burned just as we had passed through it.

Being so young, I was confused as to what was going on. There was much noise and panic. A Burmese man held a gun to my head demanding the family part with either their jewellery or their little boy. Fortunately, they chose me. The Burmese were on the side of the British until the Japanese came so I could not understand why we were being robbed by a Burmese bandit.

Setting out for the Raj which was hundreds of miles away, we kept close to the banks of the Irrawaddy. This broad river, with its source in the melting snows of the Himalayas is a natural highway. The British nicknamed it 'the road to Mandalay'. Not only do the flying fish use it as a playground, but flying squirrels use the trees along its banks as a vast circus tent in which to display their unique form of acrobatics. As this was a trek and not a package tour, no one noticed them but the kids.

1

We did not get much further than Mandalay. Just north of this ancient capital, the Japanese caught up with us and interned us for the rest of the war. The next few years are very hazy to me. My uncle, who joined us at Mandalay, was also interned with us and was beaten up and forced to live in a chicken coop. His meals were thrown to him through the wire mesh. Oblivious of their brutality, the incident that sticks in my memory is the kindness of a Japanese soldier. Somehow I reminded him of his own son back home. As a result he secretly gave me some of his rations of milk and sugar - that was like being given caviare and champagne.

Cut off from the outside world, life in the camp settled into a boring routine. Spending the next three years of my life there does not seem to have left too many scars. Perhaps it was because the camp was composed of women, children and old people that we were treated less harshly. Compared with what the Japs were doing to get the Burma railway built, this was a holiday camp. But the end was just as sweet when it came.

Unknown to us, General Wingate's teams were slipping behind Japanese lines. They did not use conventional tactics, instead they pioneered jungle warfare using guerrillas. Every war in South East Asia has employed the same tactics ever since. Known as the Chindits — after the mythological lions guarding the temples throughout Burma - they retraced the steps which the British army were forced to follow in their ignoble retreat

When the Japanese guarding our camp got wind of it they fled. When we realised what had happened no one was sure what to do. No one except my mother. She was determined to return to Rangoon where she intuitively felt she would find my father. As war was still raging further south this meant we would have to go through the frontline. Undeterred, mother disguised herself as a Red Cross nurse. Grabbing my hand she dragged me through another nightmare. To this day I can remember the stench of the dead bodies.

We reached Rangoon soon after it was liberated in March 1945. Tracing my father was a long drawn-out process. When we were finally reunited no one was more surprised than he was. He had been told we were all dead. Spending the war in India meant he never saw any action. This, added to the fact that he thought his family had been wiped out, made him turn to drink and opium.

2

My grandfather was the only one who died. Dysentery killed him just before the Japanese ran away from the camp. His death diminished me. He had taken the place of my absent father but it was more than that. The only person who really understood me had vanished to be replaced by this stranger called my father. Granddad had led a riotous life and then become a convert to the Salvation Army. When at the age of seven I went forward to one of their penitent forms, my grandmother thought I had had a religious experience. Although I was always conscious of God in an unthinking way, this spontaneous act was more an expression of my loss.

Many years later, when my gran was in her seventies she told me that she had been asking the Almighty to make me a minister of his church. Nothing could have been further from my mind at the time. 'Perhaps I will one day Gran', I said, trying to comfort her, 'When I'm your age!' The joke backfired. Before I had reached my thirtieth birthday I was ordained. Unanswered prayer would later cause me problems. However, the answered prayer of my grandmother would take a book to explain.

Back in Rangoon, the city of my birth, things were beginning to return to 'normal'. The British were climbing back into the driver's seat after their wartime hiatus. As a family, we began to hire the local people as our servants again, unaware that there was a change of attitude. Having tasted a sort of independence during the war they resented the whites taking up the reins again.

My first taste of this resentment was at school. Going to school was an alien concept to me, even though I was almost eight. Add to this the humiliation of being called a 'white monkey' and beaten up, it's easy to see why I played truant. As I spent more time running away than learning, my parents decided to send me to a boarding school. Seeing the look of terror in my face which was drenched with tears every time she visited, proved too much for my mother. She began to rethink her decision.

Luckily for me a national strike brought the country to a standstill. Burma was demanding independence. We realised that our days were numbered and started to make plans to return to England. For a century my family had links with India and Burma, mainly as part of the aggressive East India Company or as mercenaries. One of my ancestors was the captain of the main British task force which went up the Irrawaddy river to beat the Burmese into submission in the Second Anglo-Burmese War.

My father was responsible for setting up Horlicks in the country. Not only did he manage to sell it to the ex-pats, but also the natives. They loved the taste of the tablets. With him travelling the country my parents were separated for long spells. Mother coped by getting involved in lots of charitable work, Dad by bestowing his favours on the local girls. When he returned home he was full of stories about the leg-rowers of Ingle Lake or the remarkable 'giraffe women' of the Padaung tribe.

My memories are mostly about trivial things like kite fights. Delicately designed pieces of rice paper were attached to a cross-piece of light wood. The fine string which kept the kite from flying away was covered with ground glass just under the frame. By cunningly flying your kite near to another one, you could knock it out of the sky by rubbing the strings together. Dog-fights in the air often led to punch-ups on the ground.

Then there were the rainbaths. During the summer months you could bank on a daily shower every afternoon. As kids we loved running out into the rain fully clothed. The hot sun soon dried them out. It was very refreshing. The main image that remains of Burma is of the monsoon rains. To say it buckets down would be an understatement. But these rains nourish the rice crop. Rice being at the heart of the economy, the countryside was a patchwork of flooded paddy fields. Before the war, Burma was the world's largest exporter of rice.

Although the war completely devastated Burma, I was blissfully unaware of it. Life carried on as usual until my father announced that he had booked our passage back to Britain. Apparently the nationals were demanding that those who wanted to stay would have to take on Burmese nationality. To the patriotic ex-pats it was unthinkable.

On the 4th of January 1948 after almost a century of British rule, Burma declared her independence. That day we sailed out of Rangoon harbour to return 'home'. To my childish mind it conjured up pictures of Robin Hood and people speaking with clipped accents. Regional dialects were not heard on film in those days. My last sight of this mystical land was

4

of the myriad spires of the Shewdagon Pagoda. People said there was more gold on the Shewdagon than in the vaults of the Bank of England.

Sailing back to England was boring. Bingo was invented to distract the passengers. Seeing nothing but sea for days on end is very tiresome. Then one day I looked out of the porthole and saw sand. Running to the other side of the ship confirmed it wasn't a mirage. Over in the distance there was a string of camels. We were going through the Suez Canal but the sensation was eerie. Finally, after nearly a month at sea we docked at Southampton.

STRANGER IN A STRANGE LAND

My family's roots in England can be traced back over a thousand years. In the 9th century a settlement of Tarletons started just south of Preston. Various members of the family held land all over Lancashire. One of my ancestors settled in Dublin at the end of the 16th century. Around him grew the myth that we once owned a castle in Ireland. On close investigation it turned out that he merely leased Killeigh Abbey from Lord Digby.

Probably, my most famous ancestor was Richard Tarleton, the jester in Queen Elizabeth's court. Some scholars think that Shakespeare had him in mind when he speaks of poor Yorick. 'Where be your jibes now? Your gambols, your songs, your flashes of merriment, that are wont to set the table on a roar?', says Hamlet gazing at his skull. Having this wise fool in our background would account for the rich blend of wisdom and folly in our history.

Returning home was not a bundle of laughs for me. Austerity was Britain's reward for surviving World War II unbeaten. Rationing of meat, butter, cheese, tea, sugar and sweets were the hall-mark of this age of self-denial. Where were all the exotic fruits I had taken for granted? Oranges were the only fruit and they were almost non-existent.

Having lost four years of my education meant I would spend the rest of my school days trying to catch up. My parents sent me to a prep school to learn the basics, but our money ran out after six months. This forced them to send me to the local junior school in London. At the prep school the flat unmelodious vowel sounds of my colonial speech went unnoticed. But in the middle of London's East End it stood out like a sore thumb. Now I was called 'Jungle Bunny' and asked if I lived in a tree.

Immigration from the commonwealth had not really begun, so there were no black faces at school. My white face with a strange accent made me the object of incipient racism. Within months I had not only acquired a flowing cockney brogue but also became a good boxer. No one was going to beat me up as they did in Burma. Nell was the nickname I was given after Nell Tarleton. He was another one of my relatives who won two Lonsdale Belts for boxing. Unfortunately he died a month before collecting the pension that went with it.

Somehow I managed to fool the authorities into giving me a place in a grammar school. St.Marylebone Grammar was a school for boys with a tradition of over two hundred years. I was not impressed. It had the same feel to it as the Japanese prison camp. I could not wait to leave. No happy memories survive of this internment, just a few moments of laughter relieved the boredom. Like the time one of my friends was caught reading a comic in the history lesson. Protesting his innocence, he was questioned about the lesson. 'Right, Barton', said the master, 'You are a medieval farmer. You are growing wheat in this field and rye in the next, what would you do with the other field?' 'Dig a pond and keep ducks sir'. Dick Barton's anarchic spirit did not fit into this archaic system so he was expelled.

My boxing skills proved less efficient in this larger arena. Nell became Nellie. But I could still talk tough and found the tongue was mightier than the boxing glove, until I met Allan. He was a South African lad who was over six foot. Calling my bluff, he challenged me to meet him in the ring during the lunch hour the following day. Panic stricken, I turned up for the match. Half the school seemed to be in the gym to witness my humiliation. Luckily he never turned up and I learned not to boast about skills I did not possess.

However, it was the start of a fascination for those who were skilful when they put the gloves on. Boxing is barbaric. Down the years there have been many calls for the sport to be banned, some even questioning the use of the word 'sport'. Yet forty years on I am still drawn to the big fight. Even though I have seen my hero Mohammed Ali reduced to a shadow of his former glory, I am still drawn to watch.

Meanwhile my family were growing in number and poverty. Mother struggled to bring up four boys single-handed. Dad spent two years in a sanatorium fighting TB picked up in the opium dens in India, and I did my best to take his place. There were nine years separating me and my next brother so I used sheer brute force to impose my authority.

To make ends meet my mother took in home work. She would bring home garments made in the workshop and finish them off for a pittance. It was white slave labour. To make matters worse, the garments were brassieres. Wherever you looked there were mountains of them. No wonder I never invited anyone home. This was all happening at a time when I was becoming curious about what filled these curious dome-shaped structures.

Sex was kept under wraps as I grew up. Adults felt that children must be kept in the dark until they became adults. No sex education meant we were forced to learn the facts of life from dirty jokes and smutty stories. The seed that it was somehow unclean was planted in our fertile minds by a generation who knew no better. But all that secrecy was about to be blown.

The Kinsey Report was published when I was fifteen. It was a bombshell. Half the women questioned admitted to having sex before marriage. More mind-blowing was the fact that women claimed to enjoy sex as much as men. The image of women had been changed for ever. Marilyn Monroe and Brigitte Bardot did more than anyone to change the sex-as-procreation myth to the sex-as-fun. They brought to the screen an eroticism that retained a suggestion of innocence at the heart of it. The twist these two added was that they treated men as playthings.

Unaware of the changing attitudes of society, schoolboys like me just revelled in the pictures published in *Playboy*. The first issue, published in the same year as the Kinsey Report, had Marilyn Monroe as its centrefold in the notorious calendar pose. In the same year Ian Fleming introduced us to James Bond with his special brand of snobbery and violence. What made him appealing to those of us who were becoming sexually aware was not so much his licence to kill, as his licence to seduce. No wonder so many of us became male chauvinist pigs.

Single sex schools, like the one I was attending, have always left their pupils foundering when confronted with the other sex. Homosexuality was rife at St. Marylebone Grammar, but somehow I was drawn to the opposite sex despite the mystery. But my gawky response to girls forced me to retreat into shyness and fantasy while still at school.

School is an apt word for the institution I attended, for while it failed to educate me, it succeeded in schooling me. They taught me to be punctual, to do menial tasks and to submit to authority. Caning was the *modus operandi* - especially the Latin master's. Once the headmaster found one of our class who had been thrown out for misbehaving. Grabbing him by the scruff of the neck, he bent him over my desk in the front and gave him six of 'the best'. No actor could reproduce the look of fear mixed with courage on that boy's face.

Acting was my chosen profession as my school days ended. Obviously I had been in a few school plays. Once I had played the Dark Lady of the Sonnets, but then men playing women had been the custom in Shakespeare's day. Yet these failed to fire my imagination. Laurence Olivier did. Seeing him bring to life the *Hamlet* we murdered in the classroom was magical. I ran home, found the 'To be or not to be' soliloquy and learned it by heart. Olivier provided me with the key that unlocked the secrets of Shakespeare. The bard wrote for the ear and should be heard before he is read. To this day I am thrilled that he succeeded where my English masters had failed.

When I told my careers' master that I intended to be an actor, he said it was too precarious and refused to help me. My next choice was to be a journalist, but he gave up on that idea too and said it would be better if I trained as a librarian. My aim was to go to the Royal Academy of Dramatic Art but my parents couldn't afford the fees. So I left school with a handful of 'O' levels and took a job in one of the John Lewis stores while waiting for an opportunity to knock.

Looking back at my days in St.Marylebone Grammar School, I feel that religious education should be banned. What should be an affair of the heart is turned into a mind trip. While you can teach moral values - if you feel that yours are superior - it's impossible to teach what should be experienced. The nearest I came to being moved in my spirit was in assembly once a year. Being a creature of habit, the headmaster would annually read the account of Mr. Valiant-for-Truth's death from *Pilgrim's Progress*. 'And the trumpets sounded for him on the other side.' While identifying with Bunyan's hero, I had yet to find a truth to be valiant for.

CELEBRATION OF YOUTH

The Fifties was a time when it was pleasant to be young enough to be mildly rebellious. 'Teenager' was a word few people used until I was in my mid teens. On my seventeenth birthday 'Rock Around The Clock' became the anthem of all classes of dissident youth. The drum beat was like the starting pistol of a new era. Jazz had captured my heart, but this was something else. It was raw but full of life.

In an age when style would matter more than substance, Bill Haley was a disappointment in the flesh. How could this tubby, ageing man produce such a youthful sound? Later I discovered that white musicians had pinched the sound from their black brothers. Six months after their hit, Bill Haley and the Comets were eclipsed by a young man who looked the part -- Elvis Presley. He was our symbol of vitality and rebelliousness.

Before this moment you were either a child or an adult. Now there was something in between: a youth culture. For the first time you could be young and enjoy it. For the moment we were aimlessly rebelling. So when the film *Rebel Without A Cause* was released in September 1955, it was easy for us to identify with James Dean's delinquent, hurt hero. Dean embodied the sense of alienation we felt and became the role model for those of us who did not want to join the grown-up world

My enjoyment of this lively scene began to be curtailed when my mother decided it was time for me to be confirmed. Even though she rarely went to church, she-who-must-be-obeyed felt the vows made on my behalf in St.Philips' Church in Rangoon needed to be confirmed. It seemed to be irrelevant that I was not willing to renounce the world, the flesh or the devil. The world was an exciting place, the flesh of a woman was irresistible, and the devil appeared to have all the best music.

Needless to say all I felt at my confirmation was the weight of the bishop's hands on my head. But it did give the vicar a chance to call round for a chat. The Rev. Jack Hoare was a useless preacher. He made up for that with the pastoral side of his ministry. This man loved people. Despite a bad hearing loss and speech impediment which would have most people withdrawing into their own little world, he invaded our world. Using every excuse in the book to call round, Jack pestered me into

10

joining the church youth club. After the twentieth visit, I decided to give it a whirl.

To my amazement I really liked it. Expecting to be bored, I was pleasantly surprised to find a lot of fun and games. We went on rambles in the country, put on lively dances and staged plays. It was good, clean fun. The short epilogue at the end was the only spoonful of medicine we were forced to take.

Girls were the main attraction. Approaching my sexual prime meant I couldn't stop thinking about them. Here I was presented with a variety of females and the context in which to shop around. Perhaps there was a heaven after all.

Pat Dykes was the first girl I really fancied. The only problem was that a dozen other blokes did as well, so I became part of the entourage who walked her home. It is difficult to know why she attracted so much attention. She was not the prettiest girl in the club, perhaps it was the sense that she was unattainable that spurred us all on. When she finally chose me, I found that despite some passionate kissing, she was unattainable sexually.

Soon after going out together the youth club arranged a weekend away. The idea of these 'house parties' was to gather outsiders like me into the fold and challenge the backsliders. So all the interesting events were punctuated with regular doses of religious medicine. Their mission was to give us a sufficient amount of moral laxatives to purge our souls.

My mission was much simpler - to get Pat Dykes beyond the kissing stage. Unknown to me, the medicine was beginning to work on her. Imagine my surprise when she came up to my room on the first night. When I shut the door, she burst into tears. Here was the opportunity I had been waiting for. All I had to do was to give her my shoulder to cry on, comfort her and then defrost her with my charm. But when she explained the reason for her tears I was speechless.

'I am not serving God as I ought', she sobbed. What kind of dilemma was this? How could anyone cry over something as trivial as this? My limited experience of women had shown me that women tended to cry very easily. They cried not only when they were sad but also when they were happy. There was always a reason. Not serving God as one ought was not a sufficient reason even for a woman. Suddenly I was out of my depth. The language was foreign to me. Fused with emotion, it sounded to me as if came from another planet. When in doubt waffle, so I did. Shaken by the experience of a faith that could move people to tears, I decided to listen to what the leaders of the house party were saying. One verse that still lingers in my memory of that fateful weekend was from John's Epistle: 'These things write we unto you that your joy may be full'.

Joy was the last thing I thought of when religion was mentioned. Kill-joys sprang more readily to mind when thinking about Christians. 'Thou shalt not' never seemed far from their lips. Yet I had to admit that those who claimed to be Christians in this group had something I definitely lacked. When challenged about it, they said with one voice the difference was Christ. The more I looked into it, the more logical it all seemed. By the end of the house party I knew I wanted to let Him into my life. Sadly it would be many years before I would taste the joy St. John spoke of.

Entering the Evangelical fold was simple they said. 'Admit you are a sinner. Believe Christ died for you. Count the cost. Do something about it'. Admitting I was a sinner was not hard even though I had not done anything really wicked. Pat Dykes would not let me. However the church saw anything to do with sex as sinful: so sinful that any hint of it was removed from Christ's entry into the world by the clever device of a virgin giving birth. Many other religions stumbled on the same trick.

Saint Augustine, who had got it all out of his system before entering the church, said sex was allowed so long as you didn't enjoy it. Unfortunately I did. In those pre-pill days sex was mainly confined to what we called 'heavy petting' — quite innocent by today's standards. However Evangelicals branded you as a sinner not only for what you had done, but also for what you hoped to do. 'If a man looks on a woman with a lustful eye, he has already committed adultery with her in his heart.' The names of Marilyn Monroe and Brigitte Bardot cropped up often in my confessions.

Believing that Christ died for me was also made easy. Bombarded with text after text that Christ had died for the sins of the whole world, they forced me to the logical conclusion that I was no exception. There it was in black and white in 'God's Word'. That was their term for the Bible which they believed from cover to cover, maps and all. At this stage I saw no reason to question their faith in the world's best selling book.

'Counting the cost' meant you gave up the right to live your own life. What should have been more difficult was eased by my being in love with a Christian girl, I could only see the benefits at the time. 'Doing something about it' meant telling someone. When I did, most of my friends deserted me. They saw the gleam of a fanatic in my eyes. I saw the glazed look of unbelief in theirs. The cost was beginning to tell.

Another loss was my planned career. Richard Dunn, a kindly old character actor, had taken me under his wing. While he was training me to speak Shakespearean verse, he also arranged for me to audition for a part in 'The King and I'. Not quite the start I envisaged but I was thrilled.

At the same time a vicar with an unusual parish came to speak to our Youth Club. His job was to go round to all the West End theatres and chat with all the actors. They were his 'flock'. Cornering him at the end, I asked what he thought of my plans to go on stage. 'If you are strong enough to look over the edge of a precipice without losing your balance, it will be okay', he said.

Hearing those words I knew he was bringing down the curtain on my acting career, but I was too immature to admit it. Struggling with indecision, I ducked out of the audition. Richard was furious. 'What the hell are you playing at - I thought you were serious', he yelled. 'Stop wasting my time. When you're prepared to make a real commitment, come back and see me'. He had every right to be angry, I had let him down badly.

Months of confusion followed. To be or not to be. When I decided not to be the next Olivier, everyone was relieved. Looking back I can see that it was my lack of identity (normal at my age) which drove me to hide in the make-believe world of the stage. At the time I felt the precipice the vicar pointed out was called Morality. Now I know it was called Reality, I would have had a devil of a job holding on to it.

These losses were offset by a couple of great gains. First I found my partner for life. No, not Miss Dykes. After a while I grew weary of her calling the shots, and began to play the field. After going out with a string of girls, I realised there was only one attractive girl left. Dorothy Mayhew was a beautiful brunette but I had avoided her as she was a bit of a flirt - like me. Then we were thrown together in a play in which I played her husband. Being with her during weeks of rehearsals made me revise my opinion. We started to confide in each other. Her frankness was refreshing and I enjoyed her company.

She was being dated at the time by a very serious young man who was destined to become a missionary. During the Christmas dance I decided she was not cut out for the mission field. Grabbing her for the last waltz, I placed a sprig of mistletoe above her head and kissed her all the way round the hall. Imagine my surprise when I found her boyfriend had been dancing just behind us. Under his steely glare I asked her if I could walk her home.

It was the start of a great romance which has stood the test of many heartbreaking dramas. Most of the tears have been caused by people and events outside our marriage, but we have also been within a whisker of being divorced. Little did Dorothy know what she was taking on when she married me thirty-something years ago.

The other great gain was discovering my ability to communicate to more than a handful of people. Preaching was to become the tool of my trade. My apprenticeship was served dishing out the spoonful of medicine we called 'the epilogue'. No sooner had I mastered that, than the challenge came to preach outdoors. Jack Wallace, a lawyer from Lincolns Inn Field, encouraged me to give it a try. He was a big man in every sense of the word. 'A whale is only vulnerable when it gets up to spout' he roared as he mounted the soap box. With a sense of humour and a twinkle in his eye, he preached the gospel.

Then he asked me to say a few words. Mounting the collapsible pulpit, I caught my first glimpse of the crowd and froze. Everything seemed to be happening in slow motion. The seconds before I opened my mouth seemed like an eternity. But once I started there was no stopping me. Once you have preached in the open air and taken on the hecklers, the rest is a doddle. Standing in a church pulpit is standing six foot above contradiction, no one shouts you down. What a difference it would make if they did, it would inject a sense of reality into the service.

14

Obviously I was delighted when people told me my sermon had stirred them. It was good for the old ego. Yet there was something more to it than that. I felt I was doing what I was born to do - not just communicating but making people think.

One summer's night my concept of preaching was shattered. Boarding the coach we headed for Wembley Stadium, the scene of many football cup finals. As we arrived a choir of 1000 voices began singing 'This is my story, this is my song'. When I got my bearings I noticed the sacred turf had been violated. Right in the centre there was a vast canopy-covered platform, all the action had its genesis there. Now a rich baritone was singing 'How Great Thou Art'. What is more the arena was packed.

Then a tall, blond, handsome man stepped up to the microphone. His deep Southern accent was enchanting. His conviction even deeper. No man spoke with such authority and simplicity. His preaching was not something to be endured but enjoyed. Then he went too far - he invited the people who wanted to give their lives to God to join him on the turf. Maybe this kind of thing was all right for Americans, but someone should have told the man about our British reserve. Nothing happened at first. Then the odd person began to move. What started as a trickle soon became a flood. Someone should have told me this was Billy Graham's stock-in-trade. It had a profound effect on me.

VALIANT FOR TRUTH

Our fear that there was something strange about the new vicar was confirmed in the national newspapers. 'Vicar Arrests Thief at Swordpoint', screamed the headline. Apparently the unsuspecting burglar was going about his business when the minister pounced on him. Not satisfied with having knocked him to the ground, he grabbed one of the swords hanging on the wall. Holding the blade to the poor man's throat he cried 'I arrest you in the name of the Queen'. Next day the cartoonists' delight was plain to see. One had the shadow of a vicar brandishing a sword in the background. In front was a thief on his knees, pounding the door of a police station crying, 'Sanctuary! Sanctuary!'

The Rev. Jack Dover-Wellman was a one off. He was one of those eccentrics England delights in breeding. For example, he had chosen not to belong to any of the three main streams which flow through the Anglican Church. Let me explain. The high church see the Church as the fount of all wisdom. The low church claim the Bible as the final authority. In the middle are the majority who say Reason must be the ultimate judge. Jack was neither high, middle or low.

Why he chose to come to a church with a long-standing low church tradition is a puzzle. The evangelicals, to give them their other name, have always had a clear sense of what is heresy. To them 'faith' is not simply trust, it is a set of clearly defined propositions like the 39 Articles of Faith the vicar was supposed to believe. At the heart of their philosophy is the belief that the Bible is the word of God - literally. Most people would say the Bible is open to interpretation. They claim it is self-interpreting.

For some strange reason he had chosen to come among people who knew what they wanted to hear from the pulpit and would not stand for a man who seemed to be making it up as he went along. Daniel was throwing himself into the lion's den. 'We must report him to the bishop', cried these low church lions. 'The man is a heretic'. The bishop was clearly taken aback. How could anyone be charged with heresy in the Church of England? Embracing every shade of doctrine man had invented was its proud boast. 'If you want to get rid of your vicar you must take your case to an ecclesiastical court', said the bishop as he washed his hands.

16

Those who wanted a quiet life just slipped away to other churches. The rest of us decided to stay on and fight. It felt strange defending the faith against the man chosen to preach it. Until that moment the vicar seemed to be the king of the castle, we were just peasants who warmed the pews. Now the peasants were revolting. This was my first taste of anarchy. Soon the older folk realised they were beaten and withdrew. Unable to dethrone the king, the young ones set up a second court using the youth club as our base. From here we started to preach our own version of the truth.

Our leader was the only older man left. Doug Gibson was one of those strong father figures who draw people to themselves. Probably because his choice was now limited, he chose me to be his deputy. His calm response to a crisis, coupled with his commonsense approach, gave him the authority to hold it all together. After a year the verbal battles with Rev. Dover-Wellman degenerated into slanging matches. His threat of closing down the youth club hung like the sword of Damocles over our heads. So we moved the whole group to a neighbouring church, ending a valiant fight for what we saw to be the truth.

My faith in the Anglican system had been badly shaken. How could they allow this loose cannon on the deck of what had been a friendly ship? Surely bishops were there to protect the flock from false shepherds, not throw them to the wolves? Why was there no one with an ounce of Billy Graham's charisma or a fraction of his authority?

Luckily a letter from Her Majesty the Queen would distract my attention for a couple of years. She asked me to join her Armed Forces. Not conscientious enough to object, I was forced to sign up. The madness of war would one day dawn on me, but for the moment the idea of wearing a uniform had curious appeal. The discipline that went with the uniform soon killed that stone dead.

Drill instructors not only kicked and punched us into line, they also made us do mind-boggling things. After painting trees green and coal white, I realised why they say 'Bullshit baffles brains'. Sharing a bedroom with my three brothers did nothing to prepare me for the ordeal of sharing a barrack room with 24 immature males. The air was thick with blue jokes on the first night as they competed with each other for the title of Macho Man.

In that bawdy atmosphere I decided to make my stand. Kneeling by my bedside, I pretended to pray. I could not concentrate as I had heard stories of boots being hurled when others had done the same. They just ignored me. As my first effort at martyrdom had been thwarted, I jumped into bed and prayed that God would get me out of this hell hole. He also ignored me, so I decided to plan my escape from this prison myself.

Within a couple of weeks I reported to the Medical Officer as all this square-bashing (marching) was killing my feet. What I thought were chilblains turned out to be something more useful. 'You've got flat feet laddie', said the Medical Officer. 'They made a mistake when they passed you as fit, you shouldn't be in the forces at all'. That was music to my ears. Now all my efforts were channelled into getting an early discharge. However as I was 'fit' at my initial medical, this meant that I became 'disabled' during my time in the R.A.F. and they would have to give me a pension. 'I don't want a pension', I cried. 'Just get me out before I become brain dead'. They flatly refused, but I was excused from wearing boots. That meant I was not expected to keep in step with the others as I was also excused from marching.

One thing I was not excused was injections. My phobia about needles was not something I wanted the boys to know about, so I joined the queue in silence. Britain's Strongest Youth was directly in front of me. For the first three months of his National Service he never wore a uniform. They could not find one to fit him. His massive shoulders, small bum and titanic thighs split everything they gave him. In front of him was the frailest man I had ever seen; all skin and bones with no flesh. This weed did not flinch as the needle punctured him but Britain's Strongest Youth went out like a light in front of me. Laughing at the irony, I never felt a thing.

R.A.F. West Kirby was just across the water from Ireland. As the IRA lacked the funding they now have, they often had sorties on armouries like ours. We were sent out in twos at night to guard it with truncheons and torches. No one took the IRA seriously in the late fifties. We did, so we made a pact to run at the first sign of trouble. More worrying was the fact that I was given access to Secret and Top Secret documents eighteen months before they checked into my background.

My desk job was so boring I came home every weekend. One time my best friend was offered a lift home in a sports car. As he rarely went home, I pleaded with him to let me take his place. When he refused I offered him large sums of money. Although this usually did the trick, Clive refused to give me his place. What neither of us knew was that the TR2 sports car was prone to roll over. Coming back to base on Monday morning I heard that Clive was killed instantaneously as the car turned over. The driver escaped with a few grazes. Incidents like that serve as a reminder that none of us will get out of here alive.

Another time when I felt close to death in the R.A.F. was when I was taken up for a flight in a Chipmunk. Sitting in the cockpit the whole craft seemed very fragile to me. Suddenly the wheels stopped rumbling and we were airborne. Flying was a breathtaking experience. 'She's all yours', said the pilot giving me the controls. Either this man was a fool or very brave I thought, but took the chance with both hands on the joy stick. Words cannot describe the sensations I felt on that warm summer's day.

'Right', said the pilot taking back the controls. 'I need to regain the two thousand feet you lost. Now I'm up here to practice, so fasten your seat belt'. Looping the loop was fantastic at first but I began to feel queasy by the end. Then he turned the engine off. The only problem was he had not landed the plane. Thousands of feet in the air, I watched the nose drop and we plummeted toward the earth. Trust me to pick a nutter, I thought. He was not mad, just practising how to get out of a stall, but it scared the pants off me.

Every now and then someone claims that bringing back National Service would restore discipline amongst the young. That argument is as flawed as bringing back hanging as a deterrent. What most of us learned was how to avoid doing what we were told. Skiving was the name of the game. All we lived for was our time off. The camp was like a ghost town at weekends with a skeleton staff who were not clever enough to wangle a 48 hour pass. Discipline was a dirty word.

Back in civvy street I found it difficult to settle. Now that I had decided an actor's life was not for me, my life lacked direction. Nothing appealed to me, so I just drifted. Dorothy had started to work as a secretary for a large firm of hearing aid consultants. They suggested I should train as an audiologist. This meant I would test people's hearing and fit them with electronic devices where necessary. The job proved very rewarding. You enabled people to hear again and, as I was working in the private sector, it was well paid.

It is difficult to understand people trapped in that twilight zone between hearing and total deafness. The frustration was forcefully brought home to me with the first patient I dealt with. She was a jolly Welsh lady. 'Look luv', she said, 'You have got to help me, people think I'm daft. I'm not, I'm deaf and they cannot see the bloody difference'. Having a high frequency loss meant she missed bits of words. Everything was loud enough, it just lacked clarity. Today it is relatively easy to rectify that kind of loss. In the early sixties we did not have the technology, yet somehow I was able to help.

Dorothy and I were married during my last year in the R.A.F. Our first home was a one room attic flat with the landlord living downstairs. He was spooky. Every morning at about 4 a.m. he would creep out of the house to feed the local birds. The police shadowed him for weeks, believing he was involved in something more sinister. When we invited the bird-man to tea, he refused the boiled egg and said 'Just a crumb for me', and we nearly choked with laughter when he literally took two crumbs off the plate. When he heard that I could preach, he promised to send me on a world tour if I included an anti-vivisection slot when preaching the gospel. Being only vaguely aware of what it meant, I declined his offer.

Another animal lover was about to affect our lives more permanently. Dorothy's aunty Ethel had no children. All her maternal instincts were lavished on her dogs. When she died we all joked that Battersea Dogs Home would get all her money. The laugh was on us. She left her estate to be divided up among her nine nieces and nephews. Her husband, who had spent all his life working hard and saving, never lived to enjoy the fruits of his labours. We did. Perhaps he helped shape my attitude towards money. Seeing it as congealed energy, I have never seen the

20

point of saving it. Like blood, it is only useful when it is flowing in the warm arteries of life.

Money does not buy happiness but it does buy freedom of choice. Feeling hemmed in by the restrictive practices of the Church of England, and drained by our total commitment to the new youth club, we decided to get away from it all. Sunbury-on Thames was the ideal place to hide.

Initially we did not join any church group. Guilt crept in and demanded we attended a local church. After shopping around for months, we decided the local Congregational church was more to our taste. Unlike the Anglican church, the sermon was not an optional extra but the focal point. A Billy Graham type message was preached in the evening, but without any flair. No one ever responded but at least they were trying. Not wanting to get too involved we never mentioned our past roles, just warmed the pews Sunday by Sunday.

As time went by we heard the youth fellowship needed a house to meet in. Our lovely three-bedroom semi with its through-lounge was made to measure. After church the young people trooped back to our place for coffee and a chat. Soon we were back at the heart of things. 'Will you preach for me next Sunday, George?', said the minister.

Once he found that I had some ability, he decided to nurture it. Giving me more opportunities to preach was only part of the plan. He had a feel for the historical roots of the Nonconformists. 1662 was the watershed. All those who refused to conform were kicked out of the Church of England. 'There I met an old man who wouldn't say his prayers; so I caught him by his left leg and threw him down the stairs!' Goosey, Goosey Gander was not just a nursery rhyme, it was a political statement.

Nonconformity was dominated at the beginning by the Puritans. Their aim was not just moral but doctrinal purity as well. Being among the intellectuals of their time, they ended up with a cerebral form of Christianity known as Calvinism. John Calvin's fine mind gave birth to this rational form of fundamentalism. He also signed the death warrant of the man who disagreed with him. No wonder it spawned systems like apartheid in South Africa and individuals like Ian Paisley in Ulster.

After attending the wedding of a friend in Belfast, I was invited to the home of the Rev. Ian Paisley who had conducted the service. Unknown in England at the time, he was notorious in Ulster. His house was surrounded by barbed wire, patrolled by alsatians and guarded by men who looked like they were hired from the Mafia. This was before the 'troubles' started. During the meal he asked if I would say a few words at his midweek prayer meeting.

Expecting the usual handful of faithfuls, I was amazed to find over 300 people there. Paisley controlled the whole affair striding up and down the aisle, stopping people if they prayed for too long. His authority was unlike anything I had ever experienced, except when watching a sergeant major on a parade ground.

During my visit he dealt with hundreds of rioters who had gathered in the Newtownards Road. No one, including the police, were able to deal with this angry Protestant mob. Paisley spoke to them for a few minutes, asked them to join him in the Lord's prayer and led them in singing the 23rd Psalm. Then he told them to go home. Like sheep hearing the voice of their shepherd, they obeyed him. Here, I thought, was the man who could solve the smouldering crisis in Ireland. Wrong. Ian would use his oratory to fan the sparks of hatred into a bonfire of insanity.

Someone said that fundamentalism is 'no fun, all mental, and full of isms.' Calvanism is a prime example. Puritans despised all forms of pleasure. Paradoxically, when they landed in the New World they claimed the 'pursuit of happiness' was one of the rights of man. What attracted me to this hard line doctrine was it appeared to be the thinking mans answer. All other forms of fundamentalism involved a kind of intellectual suicide. Here was a logical system of belief that could be argued rationally. As my heart was not yet fully engaged, it was great to have a form of truth which didn't involve the emotions.

Retracting deeper into this ancient monument to truth that Calvin had erected, I felt very secure. Separating truth from error was a simple mental exercise. From the cerebral castle of Calvinism, I could look down on the world and feel superior. Like one of the knights of old, I would on occasions leave my impregnable castle to do battle with the heretics. Sadly, if I had met the 1990s version of myself I would have disowned me.

22

GOD'S MANDATE

Convinced that the father to be should at least suffer mentally, Dorothy's mother described in graphic detail all the problems she had bringing her four children into the world. Reduced to a nervous wreck, I began to wear out the carpet. Muffled cries percolated through the ceiling. 'It's coming', shouted the jubilant midwife, grabbing my hand and pulling me up the stairs like a little boy. My natural revulsion at seeing blood, coupled with my mother-in-law's gory tales, made me feel as if I was being punished.

Holding Dorothy's hand only served to heighten my sense of helplessness until I hit upon the idea of reading what I thought were comforting verses from the Bible to her. 'Comfort, comfort ye my people saith the Lord, she hath received double for all he sins. 'Stop, stop', groaned Dorothy, 'Its an awful passage of scripture and its not comforting me at all.'

'Labour' fails to describe what I witnessed -- courage comes closer. I felt a wimp by comparison. During the delay, I began to doubt anything would come out of that tiny opening. Then I witnessed one of nature's great miracles: the genesis of life. When my firstborn finally graced us with his presence, he was not beautiful. More like a shrunken old man than a bouncing baby boy. After hours of labour, it was all over so quickly I would have liked an action replay to savour the wonder of new birth. Four years later it happened with the birth of my daughter. Magical moments are always fleeting.

Everything was going so well. We had a nice house in a pleasant location. My job was well paid and gave me the satisfaction of helping people to hear well. The car was changed every year without fail. Our church was full of friendly caring people. Now there was this delightful bundle of life to make our joy complete. Why did I have to spoil it?

'There is no way I'm going to be a minister's wife', yelled Dorothy. 'If God has called you to the ministry, why didn't He mention it to me? Anyway I'm not going to look frumpy or tie my hair back in a bun and I will never wear a hat'. What should have been a beautiful solemn moment was fast becoming a crisis. Telling her she did not have to wear a hat seemed to add an element of farce to it.

For some time I had secretly nursed the desire to be a minister and everybody except Dorothy was encouraging me in that direction. The little church had promised to support me and my family if I decided to go to college. As all but a couple of them were just making ends meet, this was a remarkable pledge. All that was missing was some confirmation from the pages of the Bible. There was this strange concept that the inward call needed to find an echo in the pages of holy writ.

Setting myself the target of reading through the Bible in one year proved something — I get bored easily. The Bible is not a book but a library of sixty six books. Some are exciting, the majority are dull. I got bogged down in the Old Testament and when I got to Jeremiah I was not looking forward to wading through the weeping prophet. However, I was in for a surprise.

I came across these words at the beginning of Jeremiah. 'I have put my words into your mouth. This day I give you authority over nations and over kingdoms, to pull down and to uproot, to destroy and to demolish, to build and to plant'. These words leapt off the page and something stirred within me.

My complaint since becoming a Christian was that I had not felt anything. Whenever I raised this question I was told that facts, not feelings, counted. Living a new kind of life was the only proof that mattered. Somehow I was never really satisfied with that answer. Surely being 'born again' must involve more than a new set of beliefs and a cleaner lifestyle. At last I felt something. That obscure text stirred the depth of my being.

At the time I would have been shocked if I had realised that I would be involved in 'pulling down' the barriers between the sacred and the secular; 'uprooting' Christianity from its walled garden to grow it in the wild; 'destroying' the illusion that God could be captured in the pages of the Bible I loved; 'demolishing' the religious and moral framework that had distorted my idea of spirituality.

Four negatives and only two positives. 'To build' a creative Christianity that was not threatened by increased knowledge. 'To plant' a sense of mystery back into a world that had been raped by cold reason. Unaware

24

of the implications, I found my heart strangely warmed by this odd mandate. Had I been granted a glimpse of the future, I would have said 'No'. Not being ambitious, I just wanted to be the pastor of a congregation. Travel was not on my itinerary, let alone causing a stir.

Dorothy's little rebellion finally came to an end a few months later after she had faced her own battle. Suffering from a severe stiff neck which would not go away, she asked God to show her clearly what she must do about becoming a minister's wife. Imagine her utter amazement when reading the Bible that morning she came across this verse: 'They made their necks stiff because they would not obey me.' She told God she would submit but that He would have to use her just as she was, warts and all.

My managing director was not so easily convinced when I told him I was leaving the firm because God had called me to the ministry. 'You mean God spoke to you?' The tone of his voice was pure disbelief. 'If I wanted him to speak to me, what would I have to do?' he said. 'Make the time', I said defensively. He opened his diary. 'Well, let me see, I am free between two and three tomorrow'. Never lost for words, I said, 'You don't make appointments with Him, He will make a date with you in His own time'.

Choosing the college I would be trained in was another step along the road to personal anarchy. Naturally the Congregational Church wanted me to train in one of their colleges. But there was no way I would darken the doors of their 'liberal' institution. As the Bible was then my sole authority, the London Bible College was the obvious choice. It was interdenominational and part of the University of London. Now I realise it was a big mistake.

Evangelical colleges, like the London Bible College, have what is called a 'closed world view'. They see their view of the world as the only one. This simplistic approach is very appealing in a world that grows more complex by the hour. Mrs. Thatcher had a similar view which kept her in pole position in politics for over a decade. Like all fundamentalists, she loved confronting her opponents, while ignoring any valid objections they might have. Her great conviction that she was right never wavered. Fanatics are the same, anyone else's view is heresy.

As we had university exams to pass, we had a lot of heresy to study. Our tutors had a lot of explaining away to do. Take the gospels for example. Matthew invents the slaughter of innocent children in Herod's reign for which there is no historical evidence. Luke tells us Jesus was born during the reign of Herod the Great who died four years before Christ. The census he refers to could not have happened until Judea came under direct Roman rule when Jesus was six years old. The credibility of the nativity narratives began to look very doubtful.

The author of Mark's gospel did not know his way round Palestine and is ignorant of Jewish practice. He has Jesus talking about a woman divorcing her husband. This would be impossible in Jewish society where women had no rights. The whole question of what Jesus said and what the writers put in his mouth was a no go area to people like me who had placed their faith in the Bible. So I simply shut my mind to the possibility that these 'heretics' were on to something. Those of my friends who did not, had nervous breakdowns or ended up being very depressed.

The principal of the college was no help. 'You are here, ladies and gentlemen, to do one thing', said Dr. Kevin in his opening lecture. Turning to the blackboard he wrote the word 'WORK' in letters a foot high. He was a workaholic who worked himself into an early grave. Aloof and austere, he failed to give of himself. No one went to him with their personal problems. Thank God for lecturers like Owen Thomas. He was a wonderful counsellor to many. Although no one took notes during his lectures, they were an oasis in this wilderness.

My counsellors came from outside the college, both were Welshmen. Derek Swann was a great help on the practical side of being a pastor. During my time at London Bible College, I was his assistant in Ashford Congregational Church. Under his guidance I learned how to take christenings, weddings and funerals. These are known in the trade as the 'three wheelers' — people are wheeled into church usually without any previous contact with it. Early on I began to realise my lack of pastoral qualities. For example I do not suffer fools gladly and there are an awful lot of fools that a minister is required to suffer. Trusting God would sort out this deficiency with an extra dollop of grace, I concentrated on the preaching side of my task. Here Dr. Martin Lloyd Jones was my mentor.

Like hundreds of others who sat at his feet, I saw him as the fount of all wisdom.

The Doctor, as we affectionately called him, was one of the last great Welsh orators. Most of us were spellbound by his rhetoric. Seldom did he preach for less than an hour, usually explaining just one verse of scripture. Once he spoke for over an hour on the word 'therefore'. As it came at the beginning of the twelfth chapter of Romans, he cunningly used it to remind us of the previous eleven. It had taken him eleven years to expound eleven chapters. Initially I thought that he was a doctor of theology, but was pleasantly surprised to find that he had qualified as a medical doctor. While training to be a surgeon, he was called to the ministry. Bringing his diagnostic skills to bear on the Bible, he left no stone unturned. Yet he never brought his clinical detachment to question the Bible being infallible. But he did raise other fundamental issues. 'Over the next decade', he thundered from the pulpit, 'Two questions must be faced. What is a Christian? and what is the Church?' Those questions haunted me for many years. The Doctor would not have been pleased with the answers I came up with.

During the first half of my university course I had no time for questions. As my brain had not been seriously challenged for over a decade, it needed to be kick started. Languages had never come naturally to me, so learning a dead language (New Testament Greek) proved too much. At the end of the first term I could barely remember the alphabet. The Christmas break worked wonders. Soon I was thoroughly enjoying my new academic life.

Half way through my course I began to doubt the usefulness of all these intellectual mind games. 'What use will all this be when I am helping people face up to problems in the real world?' 'No use whatsoever,' replied Lloyd Jones. 'Unfortunately it's expected of you. So don't think of it as useful. Pretend you're studying maths. Just pass the exams'. Becoming as clinically detached as my mentor, I did enough to fool the university into giving me a piece of paper to stick on the wall.

27

CHURCH IS PEOPLE

All that remained was for me to find a church which would have me. While at college, the Congregational and Presbyterian Churches had merged. Instead of this giving me a bigger pond to fish in, my options were cut down. My home church (and about 50 other churches) decided to opt out on doctrinal grounds. As doctrine was the benchmark of my belief at the time, I joined the rebels. With only a handful of the remaining Congregational churches needing ministers, I resigned myself to looking after one of those tiny churches which cannot afford a full-time pastor.

'I have given your name to the church secretary at Chingford Congregational Church', said the college busybody. Not wanting to be under any obligation to him, I said I would think about it. On investigation, Chingford turned out to be one of those dormitory towns on the edge of London where people came home to sleep after work. Eastenders often used to retire to this town on the edge of Epping Forest.

I decided to 'preach with a view'. A strange phrase meaning you preach with view to being the next minister. If the congregation like you, at a later date you are asked back to preach again and meet with the leaders. If they like you, the job is yours. What a precarious way of choosing the man to lead you spiritually. All you need is a couple of good sermons and a nice personality to get the job. However what you need in practice is the patience of Job, the wisdom of Solomon, the intellect of Paul and the bloody-mindedness of Peter.

On the first Sunday the congregation and I 'viewed' each other, there were about 30-40 people there. Only two caught my eye. One looked like she had a bad smell under her nose, the other just beamed at me. So I preached my heart out to the radiant one. She turned out to be one of the church's missionaries back on leave from Taiwan. Second time around she had vanished and I was left with old prune face. Desperately looking for a friendly face to preach to, I saw Andy Milliken smiling up at me.

Over the next five years Andy would be my greatest ally. Being a press relations man, he helped knock some of the rough edges off me. He also acted as a buffer between the old guard in the church and the young upstart they had chosen to be their pastor. Later we found we had a lot in common. We were both imprisoned by the Japs in Burma. Andy's

28

experience was more horrific. He was forced to build the Burma railway where so many people lost their lives that each sleeper on the track was like someone's grave stone.

In the middle of this Hell-hole, Andy started to read the Bible his mum had popped into his knapsack. One day a verse jumped out of the page. As it mentioned forty-two weeks, he took it to indicate when the war would end. Everyone laughed at him. Yet the war ended exactly when he predicted - to the day.

Another ally was, strangely enough, the previous pastor of the church. Lance Vinall had served this congregation faithfully for many years, but as he was now over seventy, he felt he should retire. Instead of moving away he decided to become part of the church he had served. The combination of wise old man and young know-it-all fresh from college, looked like a disaster waiting to happen. It was not. He turned out to be a wonderful counsellor to us. I did not always understand his wise sayings. 'The Holy Spirit never ties up the loose ends', he once said. In my arrogance I put it down to age taking its toll. My views were so neat and tidy there were no loose ends. Time has proved him right, this book is full of loose ends. Lance had suffered from a heart complaint and one morning he died peacefully sitting up in bed reading his Bible.

My ordination to the ministry and my installation as the pastor of the church were two halves of the same coin. Dr. Martin Lloyd-Jones gladly accepted my invitation to preach at the ceremony. Being a bit of a rebel himself he was delighted to take part in the first ordination outside the official denomination. He used the occasion to endorse the challenge to the status quo. Rousing hymns were sung, earnest prayers were said and hands were laid on yours truly. This time I felt something more than the weight of human hands.

The new church building was typical of any nonconformist structure. Nothing fancy, just a place to meet in. But it had never been more than half full. Now they were standing in the aisles. The Doctor rose to his feet. 'Today we have not only confirmed your call to the ministry, we have joined you to this church in marriage'. Because the great man had said it, I had no intentions of ever divorcing myself from these people.

Although wearing a preaching gown was optional, I wore one from my first Sunday in the pulpit. The idea was that it gave me some sort of dignity. That illusion was shattered as I swept into the church one morning and, in a loud stage whisper, Bill cried out, 'Ere comes Batman'. This comment marked the end of my gown phase and the beginning of my decline into blazer and slacks.

Bill had spent most of his formative years in prison, mainly because he kept trying to run away. As nothing could deter him, the Governor gave in. 'Look, if you want to escape again just tell me. I'll give you a map, a packet of sandwiches and a 24 hour start'. The challenge proved too much to resist. Before the time limit had expired, Bill returned. The thrill had vanished. When he had served his time, Bill came to stay with us in the Manse.

Our first man-to-man chat took me by surprise. 'There will come a time when the desire to go back inside will be hard to fight', he said. 'It's then I'll need your help'. Having spent most of his time trying to escape from prison, I could not understand why he wanted to go back. 'I know where I am inside. Out here I have to make choices all the time', explained Bill. Inside granite walls clearly marked out his boundaries. Boring though the days were, the routine never changed. Strange how the sense of the familiar keeps us all from living unfettered lives.

'Pastor, you are a Pharisee'. Although there was no malice in her voice, Molly's calm words stunned me. There was no mistaking what she meant. How many times had I thundered out from the pulpit against the Pharisees. 'Not only do they live by the letter of the law, they are hypocrites'. Molly's sensitive spirit had picked up the legalistic way I interpreted the Bible. She also picked up that something had happened to me that I was not sharing with the congregation. More about that in the next chapter.

Molly's intuitive side had been developed over the years. It was the only way she could communicate with her eldest son John. His brain was burned out when he was only two years old. Nothing prepared me for my first encounter with him. 'His mental age is nine,' Molly told me as she took me to see John on his 21st birthday. But that was the least of his problems. His legs were deformed and he needed help getting around, while his arms seemed to have a life of their own. The only sounds his distorted face could utter made him sound more like an animal than the human being he clearly was.

Yet this remarkable woman refused to let anyone else look after him until she had a breakdown. Forced to part with him, Molly took him to his ward in South Ockendon. 'You can't put him in there. They're much worse than my John'. In that moment Molly came to terms with the size of the problem she had been grappling with. There is something unfathomable in the way the human spirit rises in a disaster that makes you proud to be human.

What also surprised me was finding out that Laurie, another member of the church, visited South Ockendon regularly. About a thousand people with mental and physical handicaps were crammed into this man-made village. Every Sunday this rather aloof man brought a team of people to Ockendon from the church. Only the service there was a lot more fun than anything they endured under my leadership.

Fully grown men, with the mental age of young boys, would come and sit on Laurie's knee and fling their arms around him. They loved him. Some of them would run around during the service shouting 'Bang! Bang!', pretending to be Cowboys and Indians. It was a revelation seeing this unemotional man throw away his mask. There was nothing patronising, just the warmth of someone who cared deeply. Communication between him and his audience was immediate. At the end of the service, they swamped him with endless cuddles.

People like Molly and Laurie were challenging me to change my persona. Unlike Laurie, I never discarded my aloofness. Thinking it was part of the job, no one was allowed to get too close to me. Although I had abandoned the preaching gown, I was clutching on to my dignity. The shroud of respectability was stifling my desire to change. Like the gown, it had to go.

Nora was one of those larger than life Eastenders. She and her husband produced five strapping kids. 'When I took Fred, I took all that came with him', she often said. Behind her big, jolly woman image she hid a sharp mind. Nora was the first to cotton on to my change of direction. 'If you had your way you'd tear the church down and start again wouldn't you?' Taken aback by her bluntness, I smiled sheepishly. 'I knew you were trouble when I first saw you', she said. 'If I had not been so soft, I should have voted against you coming here.' The laughter in her voice softened the blow. She forced me to face the issue I had been ducking. What was so wrong with the church that I couldn't conceal my desire to dismantle the whole thing?

Although there were great individuals, there was no sense of cohesion. Cliques abounded, like the choir. 'When the devil fell from heaven, he dropped into the choir stall,' I once heard someone say. They were the first line of resistance to any change. My first faltering step toward change seemed so small -- except to the choir. Most hymns in Congregational Praise failed to live up to the name. Once you eliminated the dirges, you were limited for choice. To expand my range, I decided to go for a Pentecostal hymnbook. One book was blue, the other red.

Andy was my co-conspirator in trying to change things. Knowing the hassles of getting the church to pay, he decided to pay for the new red book out of his own pocket. His generous gesture was not appreciated - especially among the choir. Throughout my remaining years at the church, it was constantly the source of heated debate. But when I left they only used the red book.

The controversy over the red and blue books puzzled me. Some of the radical things I said in the pulpit hardly raised an eyebrow. Why all the fuss about hymnbooks. Gradually it dawned on me. They did not mind me talking about anything under the sun, just as long as I did not do anything about it. Changing hymnbooks was the first sign that things could change.

My first problem was that there was nothing to bind us together. The local community were not saying 'Look how these Christians love one another', as they did with the early church. No, the only unifying factor was that we met in a building at 11 a.m. and 6.30 p.m. every Sunday. We had rightly transferred the title 'church' to the building. At least the bricks were held together with mortar. No such bonding had taken place amongst us, especially as the church was now growing in numbers.

My next problem was with worship -- or rather the lack of it. The prophet of evangelicalism, A. W. Tozer, said that worship was its missing jewel. During my time at college, I had feasted on the writings of this man.

Tozer had a very fresh way of looking at things that gave you a whole new perspective. His book on the nature of God introduced me to the mystics, for which I am eternally grateful. Probably because of his love of mysticism, he concluded that the Bible-loving community he served worshipped the Bible rather than the God it revealed.

Trying to find time to worship in the so-called Free Church service is impossible. Free they are not. Ritual dictates here as strongly as it does in the Established Church. You have the hymn-prayer-hymn-reading-hymn-sermon-hymn routine. Break that and the congregation is at a loss to respond. How could I restore the precious gem of worship into this rigid structure?

Luckily the matter was taken out of my hands. During one of our normal communion services - where there is room for a few moments of silence - a young girl started to sing 'When I survey the wondrous cross'. Slowly a few joined in. The trickle became a stream, the stream a quietly flowing river. A golden silence fell on us all as the singing stopped.

Strange how something so innocent could cause such a stir. Some of the older members felt it was an invasion of their privacy. Silence only should reign as they thought about Christ's sacrifice. The resistance movement began to gather pace. The matter would be raised at the next deacons' meeting. But as nothing was decided at that meeting about how to deal with spontaneity, we continued to push out the boundaries. Little by little we began to free the service from its hidden chains and release the bird of freedom in our midst.

Whilst communal life at South Chingford Congregational Church was a bit of a disaster, many individuals blossomed. Lily Gander was one. She thrived on challenge. Her Cockney accent and East End sense of humour added something to this very middle-class institution. However, when she prayed, she dropped her native accent in favour of a posh one. It was as though the Almighty would not grasp her rhyming slang. With that one exception, Lily was like a dose of salts among those of us who were emotionally constipated.

But one time she went too far. Returning from a meeting where she heard someone testify to having their sight healed, she smashed her specs. 'Well, that's what the Lord told this woman to do', she said 'And it worked'. When I asked her what the Lord had specifically told her to do, she admitted He had not given her any specific instructions. 'But I know He will reward my act of faith'. He did not. After a few weeks of burying her face in her hymnbook in a desperate attempt to read the print, I suggested she bought a new pair of glasses.

Soon we would all begin to learn there was a dividing line between faith and presumption. But for the moment Molly's calm statement that I was a hypocrite was haunting me. Something had happened to me while at college that had changed my life. Because of its mystical nature, I had only shared it with the few people I could trust. Even now, as I attempt to put my experience into words, I am aware that it will, in some measure, die on the page. Experience has a dynamism all of its own which gets lost in the record. That is probably why Jesus never wrote a book.

SHOCK TO THE SYSTEM

Because of my single-minded devotion to the right wing of Christianity, I wrote off the Sixties revolution as the work of the devil. Sadly those who experienced it have also written it off as a hiccup in history. As some of them now have jobs in the establishment they once despised -- especially the media -- they are embarrassed by their past.

Something happened in those years that is difficult to explain. Letting your heart rule your head is mind-blowing, especially for men. Unfortunately drugs formed the springboard for much of what happened. But to blame dope for everything is a bit far fetched. 'The evil which men do lives after them, but the good is oft interred in their bones', so let it be with the Hippies.

However I did not escape the breath of fresh air that was blowing through the world in the Sixties. The same wind blew through the church. Later they named this wind the 'Charismatic Movement', but when I was at college it was too vague to pin down. For me it all started when I read a paperback called *The Cross and The Switchblade.*

The story centred around a country preacher called to work with the street gangs of New York. Not only did he care deeply about the drug addicts, he also claimed to free the majority of them from their habit. This dimension of power made the gospel he preached good news. My gospel was bad news. 'You sin and enjoy it', I seemed to be saying, 'Become a Christian and you will still sin, but you won't enjoy it any more'. Yet here was a man claiming that bad habits can be broken, even the most binding.

Unfortunately the author of the book put his success down to being 'filled with the Spirit'. He would, I thought. Being the pastor of a Pentecostal church, he was bound to plug their pet doctrine. Believing this teaching, coupled with 'speaking in tongues', made the Pentecostals stand out like a sore thumb from the other Evangelicals. Later I discovered that speaking in tongues was not as spooky as it sounds. It simply means speaking in a language you have never been taught, a God-given language.

To my cynical mind it all seemed like religious mumbo-jumbo. Throwing it into the dustbin, I set off for my weekly fix of sound doctrine from my mentor. 'This week', said Dr. Martin Lloyd-Jones, 'We will start to deal with what people call being filled with the Spirit'. Good, I thought, that should put the lid on it. Far from confirming my glib rejection, the good Doctor set about proving from Scripture and the lives of my spiritual heroes that there was something to this strange teaching.

Six months later Dr. Lloyd-Jones was still explaining the experience of being filled with the Spirit. To him this was no optional extra. 'Speaking in tongues' was voluntary, but this was vital. 'It is your birthright', he declared. 'Go and claim your inheritance.' That was much easier said than done. 'Before you can be filled, you must be emptied', was the only pointer he gave to us.

Months of confessing and turning away from sins (real and imaginary) followed. After a while I ended up with nothing to confess. In a guilt-ridden system one feels guilty about not feeling guilty. 'Lord forgive my pride for thinking I have lived this day without sin', I cried in my despair. Not only was I praying, I was also fasting. Somehow I felt that going without my food would build up enough Brownie points to merit being filled with the Spirit. Nothing happened. The heavens were as brass.

Being religious meant I confused being upright with being uptight. The only place I really relaxed was in the bath. One day I was in the bath, with my mind in neutral, when something happened. The noise of living drowns out the still small voice of that other dimension. We live at the cross-roads of time and eternity. Suddenly this other world invaded my time zone.

Yet there was more than a sense of the eternal, I became aware of a Presence. So tangible was this other 'person' that I instinctively looked for a towel to cover my nakedness. All very embarrassing. Why could this not have happened when I was praying and fasting? Then, laughing at the stupidity of my reaction, I just laid back and enjoyed the rapture of an encounter with God. God is just a name we give to an idea, but it refers to something or someone who transcends all thought.

Sadly, when we use the word 'God' we are rarely talking about the reality the word expresses, but about the mental image that word conjures up. As language is a purely symbolic system, words only come alive when there is some kind of experience to back them up. Now eternity had come crashing in and 'God' was a much bigger word than I had ever imagined. For the first time the word 'Father' seemed the most natural way of addressing this Being.

Please forgive me if, from time to time, I call God my Father. I am claiming no special relationship as he is your Father as well. Some have yet to discover that for themselves. Jesus is not the only way to God, but he was the first to point the way to the Father. 'No one comes to the Father except by me', He said. How appropriate that the Son of man should reveal the Father in heaven.

Another thing that Jesus said is that the wind, like the Spirit, blows where it wills. 'You will hear the sound of it but you do not know where it comes from or where it is going. So is everyone who is born of the spirit'. The Spirit is as unpredictable as the wind. Jesus says that this anarchy is built into those who are filled with the Spirit. So my predictable little life was about to be turned upside down.

Having had such an experience, it is sad to report that the joy only lasted for a day. Within 24 hours this child-like moment was thrown out with the bath water of doubt. Ironically the main reason for rejecting my experience was because I didn't speak in tongues. Sharing my secret with the only person in the college who should have understood proved fatal. As a Pentecostal pastor he judged my simple little experience as not being the real thing. No 'tongue' meant there was no objective experience. He was intoning the usual evangelical line about the internal needing the external. It is a killer. Later I put this concept to death for murdering one of the most beautiful moments of my life.

While I was having my God-in-the-bath experience, a young curate from All Souls church began to write little booklets about it. The church is situated next to the BBC in Langham Place in the heart of London. An ideal place to start broadcasting what would become known as the Charismatic Movement. The Rev. Michael Harper was an excellent writer but a poor speaker. Funny how God should use such an uncharismatic man to proclaim this new dimension of the Spirit in England.

On second thoughts perhaps it was not. What was curious about this movement was its initial lack of leadership. All over the world people were being filled with the Spirit, some without even asking for it. Something spontaneous was happening. Crossing the man-made divisions we call denominations, it began to spread into the most unlikely places.

Back in those days we never realised that we were in at the start of anything so grand. Unaware of what was happening around the world, we were dismissed as Neo-Pentecostals. As we appeared to have a lot in common, Michael Harper set up a meeting with the leaders of one of the Pentecostal denominations. For some reason I was invited. Probably because I was the only Nonconformist minister at that time who admitted to being filled with the Spirit. All the rest were Anglicans.

The meeting was a disaster. Precious time was squandered debating the 'tongues issue'. One wise old man whispered something strange in my ear. 'We have wasted a day discussing two words - "must" and "may"'. Then the penny dropped. Our side argued that people filled with the Spirit MAY speak in tongues. The other side insisted tongues were a MUST. These leaders of the last wave of the Spirit were too set in their creedal concrete to see that God might be on the move again. Seeing their arrogance, I vowed to keep all my options open.

My claim that 'speaking in tongues' was an optional extra was not because of my lack of experience. By the time this meeting took place, I was using this gift regularly. But my case demonstrated that there was no connection. Some eighteen months after being filled with the Spirit, I spoke in tongues. Part of the reason for the delay was the whole thing seemed weird to me. Somehow I felt I would be taken over and made to utter gibberish.

In the end it turned out to be simply speaking in a language that was unknown to me. For someone who had been thrown out of the Latin class and failed to master French, speaking in a language whose grammar and syntax was irrelevant was a delight. Far from being taken over, I controlled the flow of this new language. The strange thing was that my mind was not involved in the speaking, so it started to criticise what was coming out of my mouth.

Before that moment, my prayer life had become so boring that I often fell asleep. To keep myself awake, I forced myself to speak out loud. But I still dozed off from time to time. God only knows what He did. After one of these little lapses, I woke up and found the language flowing from my lips was not English. In the background I could hear Dorothy calling me for breakfast. But I did not want to stop as I had no idea how to start again.

Luckily I found you did not have to drift off to use this new gift, you just had to speak out. Over the past 25 years I have found it a great way of talking to my Father. Many times I have been lost for words to describe my inner feelings. Now I have a language to express the inexpressible. Also, in some inexplicable way, you feel it somehow recharges your spiritual batteries.

Speaking in tongues is one of the many gifts of the Spirit. The Greek word for these gifts is 'charismata' meaning grace gifts. In other words there is nothing you can do to earn them, not even prayer and fasting. The Charismatic Movement is the name they gave to the restoration of these gifts to the Church. Millions around the world in the traditional churches are involved in it - even the current Archbishop of Canterbury. But when I started thirty years ago, only the Pentecostals believed they existed.

My problem was how to introduce these alien gifts into a local church which was smugly satisfied with our growing numbers. Add this to my other two problems; lack of any real sense of community and the lack of any true worship and you begin to see why I wanted to pull the thing down and start again. Lacking the courage to be that radical, I decided to renew what was there. But where does one start? Once again the matter was taken out of my hands.

CHARISMATIC CAPERS

Graham had been in college with me. Half way through his degree course he opted out and became a journalist on the local paper. Many good things would result from his being there, not least was his introducing me to squash.

'I have just discovered this game which only takes half an hour, yet you feel like you've played two hours of tennis', he said. Perhaps 'discovered' was too strong a word, but twenty years ago only the privileged few played. What Graham discovered was that it was now about to burst into the public domain.

Standing on the court with a couple of warped squash rackets, I asked him what the rules were. 'I don't have the faintest idea', said Graham, 'I just wrote about the way the game is becoming very popular.' Looking at the box on each side, the line on the front wall and the scuff marks on the sides, we made it up as we went along. As it turned out, we were not that far out. What a strange sight it must have been to anyone in the gallery. To this day I have never read the rules or had a lesson but I love the game and play regularly.

One Sunday, after the evening service, Graham burst into my vestry. He had been to a Pentecostal meeting and asked for the minister to lay hands on him to be filled with the Spirit. (Putting your hands on the head of the person asking for help was the *modus operandi*.) But the man had demanded that Graham should agree that he would speak in tongues as the 'proof' that something had happened. As he was a disciple of Lloyd-Jones, like me, he could not.

'George, I want you to lay hands on me instead', he said. Never having laid hands on anyone in my life, I was a bit non-plussed. But he insisted there was nothing to it, so I gave in. To my utter amazement he started speaking in tongues while I was still praying for him. He was doing it not because he had to but because he wanted to. Not knowing what to say I joined in using my new language for the first time in public.

Now there was no stopping him. Graham was one of these hyper-spiritual people who make me slightly uneasy. Difficult to put your finger on it, except to say there is an intensity that appears to be deep devotion. When he started to press me about using the other gifts of the Sprit in the Church, I told him the people were far from ready. As anarchy is built into being filled with the Sprit, he took no notice.

At the next mid-week meeting, he 'prophesied'. No, he did not foretell some future event, but just spoke out as if God was speaking. In the early days these prophesies were prefixed with the words 'Thus saith the Lord', which gave them an authority they did not warrant. Although I have to admit on that occasion there was that intuitive sense that God had spoken. After a few minutes I began to panic. It was all out in the open now and I would have to nail my colours to the mast.

The following Sunday I began to expound Paul's first letter to the Corinthians. Starting at chapter twelve I went through to fourteen. Most people are familiar with chapter 13 where Paul eulogises about love. But to take that chapter by itself is to lick the jam from the sandwich. Paul starts this section off with the words 'About the gifts of the Spirit..' After his poem on love he says, 'Put love first; but there are other gifts of the Spirit at which you should aim also, and above all prophesy.' Now I publicly declared that this was my aim for the local church.

No sooner had I said that than Gerry came knocking on my vestry door. 'Pastor, I believe God wants to heal my back'. He had a simple, childlike trust in God. Sorry to say I didn't, so I called Andy Milliken in to help me. 'All we have to do is to lay hands on him and leave the rest to the Lord', Andy reassured me. The next week Gerry took me to one side and said 'I have thrown away my pills!' Remembering Lily and her glasses, I cautioned him not to be too hasty. He was taking eight pain killers a day to take away the pain. But Gerry would have none of my caution. Pointing to the hill outside the church, he said 'I'll race you up that any time you like', While I was delighted for him, I was ashamed of my unbelief.

Claiming people get healed always raises the question of proof. A defence mechanism within us is triggered by such claims. If it turns out to be true, one feels their whole belief system is challenged. Perhaps that should read 'unbelief system'. Mine certainly was. Medical proof is hard to come by. When someone is healed, they claim that the original diagnosis was wrong or it is simply a remission. Gerry's remission lasted for the rest of his life as far as I know.

Stranger stories than Gerry's will follow. So let me make it plain that I'm not asking you to change your beliefs, just suspend them as you would when watching a drama on stage. At the end you can judge for yourself. Your judgement is not important to me as I no longer pray for the sick in this way. But it would be false to omit them from my story as they were real to me at the time. More importantly, they were very real to the many who experienced a dramatic change in their bodies.

Take Mrs Dewdney. She had suffered from a skin complaint for many years. Only her family knew about it, as she wore gloves outside the home. Doctors tried every form of prescription over the years but with no success. Mrs. Dewdney had one of the saddest faces I have ever seen. On Easter Sunday she popped into the vestry to ask if Andy and I would 'anoint her with oil' as she felt the Lord wanted to heal her. While it made a change from the hands-on approach we had adopted, I didn't know what to do with the oil. Settling for putting a drop of olive oil on her head, we again asked our Father in heaven to intervene.

Early the next morning she was knocking at the door of the Manse. Her sad face was now radiant. 'Pastor, look at me 'ands', she cried, 'And me feet are just the same.' She told me that during the night there had been a burning sensation throughout her body. 'When I woke up this morning me skin was just like a baby's'. Certainly there was none of the scarring she had shown me the previous night. Her family were so convinced they had witnessed a miracle, they came to church en block. Slowly it began to dawn on me that healing was something ordinary people could experience today.

Healing became a normal part of church life. Even the kids in Sunday School were asking us to pray for some sick friend or relative. Now I began to swing in the direction of believing that everyone should be healed. With God all things seemed possible. Something happened that stopped me dead in my tracks. My son Mark was diagnosed as a chronic diabetic when he was five years old. He had become listless, lost weight and was constantly going to the loo. These were all the classic signs of this disease, although we did not know it at the time. He was hospitalised immediately.

The doctors said that when they had got Mark 'balanced', he would be allowed home, but from now on would have to be injected daily with insulin. We were shattered. I now had to face my phobia of needles. Ducking the issue, I suggested to Dorothy that Mark should choose who should inject him thinking it would almost certainly be her.

Dorothy was better than me in this crisis. She practised injecting fruit and pieces of meat and even asked if she could practice on me. 'No way', I said, so she practised on her own arm. When Mark came home from hospital he said that he wanted me to inject him and he turned out to be as brave as his mother. After a month I began to wonder what all the fuss was about.

Before he left hospital, I became utterly convinced that God was going to heal him. Secure in my belief, I started to map out the book I was going to write about his healing. The book has never been written as Mark has never been healed. Why were some healed and others not? Before this moment I had always put it down to lack of faith. But now that excuse seemed lame. I decided to investigate why people were not healed. Of course I never found the answer, but my research threw up a curious fact.

Only one in ten people are healed, not only in my little church, but wherever the sick are prayed for. Many are helped, but very few are healed. This odd fact would, after many years, bring my healing ministry to a grinding halt. While it was great to see ten people healed, my heart went out to the ninety who were not. Even seeing some major illnesses cured, did not prevent that sinking feeling for the unhealed. Some were clearly disappointed, others were disillusioned.

What really hurt was seeing people chiding themselves for not having enough faith. Surely we only needed faith like a grain of mustard seed? Where was the dividing line between faith and presumption? Faith began to seem like some magical ingredient that the lucky 10 per cent stumbled on.

Luckily for me an American woman called Ann White came across my path. She claimed she would teach me to 'heal the memory'. What she meant was how to release people who were trapped by their past. The memory of all we experience is retained at a level we are unaware of. Traumatic and tragic events may fade from our consciousness, but they remain indelibly engraved at a subconscious level. Like the black box on an aircraft, all the past data can be recalled to give us a clue to what went wrong.

Ann White was riddled with arthritis. She asked the normal question 'Why me?' To her utter amazement God answered. Not with a voice that thundered from the sky, but the still small voice within that is normally drowned in the noise of daily living. 'It is because you have never really forgiven your mother'. They had never got on and over the years the resentment had built up. Now the Surgeon had put his finger on the painful spot.

Forgiveness was not easy. Gradually she began to release her mother from the bitterness that had built up within her. Bit by bit the stiffness in her joints began to ease until she was completely free from this crippling disease. Not all arthritis is cured so easily, but it was clear that forgiveness was a key.

Many problems from the past revolve around someone rather than some thing. Someone continually put you down, or hit you, or abused you. One woman I counselled suffered badly from claustrophobia. This was the result of her father locking her in a shed for hours on end when she was only four years old. When she forgave her father, her claustrophobia went out of the window. For the first time in my life I came to see how practical Jesus' teaching on forgiveness was. It was always the 'right' thing to do, now I discovered it was the healthy thing to do. Forgiving someone was not some pious act, but a very down to earth deed.

During my counselling of hundreds of people I found another key which shook my tiny Protestant mind. People needed absolution. They not only needed to forgive others, they needed to forgive themselves. Most of all they needed to know that God had forgiven them. Absolution is the ceremonial way of doing that. Stripping away the ceremony, I pronounced them forgiven in the name of the Father who I knew loved them no matter what they had done.

Most religions promote guilt as a way of trapping their followers. Many should carry the warning: 'This religion may seriously damage your health'. The West's literature is guilt-ridden as it is steeped in twenty centuries of Judeo-Christian thought. Unfortunately the majority of early Christians swallowed the Jewish lament of 'guilty before the law'.

44

Believing that Christ had died for the sins of the whole world, they should have rejected it. For, if true, there is no sin which cannot be forgiven.

As Judaism has no saviour, guilt is the main part of its ethos. Riding on the back of Christianity, it has transmitted its guilt complex to the West. The appeal of Woody Allen is that he mines this rich vein of condemnation. You may find his films very funny, but in real life a lack of self esteem is crippling.

Guilt is religion's lethal weapon. Its priests rub your nose in the dirt, then claim that their brand of soap is the only one to wash you white enough for their god. Guilt is brought about by having an unattainable moral law. Everyone is trapped. In mythology there is a dragon which has 'Thou shalt not' written on every scale of its body. Fancying myself as Saint George, I set out to slay the Law Dragon.

DEALING WITH THE DEVIL

It was nearly midnight when the 'phone rang. 'We have a boy here in the hospital who has been in a trance state for the last three days', said the policeman. 'No one can get through to him. Can you help?' Being a Christian from one of the local churches, he had heard of my work in this area. Minutes later I was bombing up the road in a police car, fulfilling a boyhood ambition.

The young man was lying on a bed in casualty. His eyes were staring blankly up at the ceiling and his hands crossed over his chest. Before doing anything, I wanted to speak to his parents. I found his father locked away in another room. When they had decided to bring the boy to Whipps Cross Hospital, he had become violent. 'When we got here he went berserk', said the bewildered father. 'He clawed his brother to the ground and ran off into the night'.

When the police finally caught up with him, he claimed to be Jesus at first and then Moses. Trying to find the cause of his trance, I asked what happened three days ago. 'Well, my son and some of his friends were mucking about with a ouija board when all of a sudden...' This was becoming a familiar story. Happily the boy was released from the grip of spirits within five minutes.

The damaging effect of playing with a ouija board was something I stumbled across. The local headmaster asked me to help out with one of their Religious Education classes. What I did not realise was they were lumbering me with a class full of drop-outs. The first lesson proved to me they were not interested in any lessons, let alone religious ones. They were waiting, like prisoners, to finish their compulsory schooling.

Discussing what they wanted to discuss was the only way to hold their attention. Ranging from the latest James Bond movie to the threat of nuclear war, I was amazed at what I was able to slip in. One day they began talking about the spirit realm. To my amazement they were very aware of this strange dimension. They told me they had been messing around with 'the spirit of the glass' and were frightened by the results.

They had arranged the letters of the alphabet in a semi-circle with the words 'yes' and 'no' at either end. Turning a tumbler upside down in the middle of the table, each participant placed a finger on the glass. Then the 'spirit of the glass' was asked to move the tumbler. Usually this spirit is only too willing, but each player thinks someone else is pushing it. So these kids set out to prove it was not a hoax by setting the spirit impossible tasks.

After some initial success, the rogue of the class decided to ask for something a bit more daring. 'We want you to break Mike King's leg', said Gough. The glass shattered. After a few minutes they were starting to laugh it off as mere coincidence. Then they heard the sound of an ambulance. Rushing over to the other side of the school, they arrived in time to see the unfortunate Mike King being carted off to hospital. He had apparently suddenly fallen head over heels down the school stairs and broken his ankle. They never fooled around with the glass again.

Lily, the one who smashed her glasses, knew some of her relatives often played this game. Popping in to see one of them, she found to her dismay that they were in the middle of a session. Refusing to go into the same room, she decided to pray in the next room against what she thought to be evil. Several unsuccessful attempts by her relatives were made to move the glass, but nothing worked. Finally, exasperated, they asked the glass the question 'Why can't we get through tonight?' The glass spelt out 'Lily'.

Technically, I also believed in a spirit realm because Jesus cast out demons. Believing is one thing, acting out your beliefs is a different ball game. Events conspired to force me into following in Jesus' footsteps in a way I had never dreamt of. Looking back, my first exorcism seems distinctly odd. Today there are many books on the subject. All we had to go on was the Bible. As it was describing events that happened 2000 years ago, there was no guarantee it would work today.

While interviewing a young couple about their marriage plans, the young woman confided she had a strange spiritual problem. Whenever she prayed she saw this 'dark angel' on the mantelpiece. Initially I dismissed it as her mind playing tricks. But she insisted she was now controlled by this 'presence'. Not knowing how to handle the situation, I asked her to come back in a week while I thought about it.

Dorothy and I sat up in bed that night going through the New Testament. What did Jesus do when he was confronted with anything demonic? He commanded it to 'go'. This was all we could find, so we decided to do the same thing when we saw the girl again. When the day came, Dorothy got scared and decided to go out for the evening leaving me to it. She felt that whatever was cast out would have to go somewhere and would probably end up in the cat. She had visions of it running up and down the curtains.

Pretending to be brave, I went over the case with the girl and read out passages of scripture where Jesus dealt with the demon. My fear manifested itself in verbal diarrhoea. I kept on talking about what I was going to do but did not get around to actually doing it. When Dorothy crept back in later that evening she found to her dismay that they were still here. Plucking up courage, we both demanded the dark angel to leave.

Nothing happened. The cat was snoozing by the fire unmoved. The girl did not feel anything either. Not knowing what to do, we told her to come back again next week. She reported that the black angel had gone but that she now felt empty inside. So we prayed for her to be filled with the Holy Spirit and, as far as I know, the dark angel never returned.

Not all exorcisms were as serene as my first. In fact they were often very rowdy events, like the time I was leading the congregation in prayer in the Anglican church in Chigwell. While the singing was more lively than one would expect in a staid Anglican set-up, nothing prepared me for the scene that followed. 'Why don't you fuck off!' shouted someone. Swearing doesn't offend me but the source was unbelievable. Opening my eyes, I saw this blue-rinse lady who looked like the chairman of the Women's' Institute. She was the picture of respectability.

Realising we were not dealing with flesh and blood here, I commanded the spirit to be silent. The torrent of words stopped. But before anyone knew what was happening, the woman attempted to strangle the man next to her with his tie. Four men were now doing their best to hold her down. Eventually she was brought into the vestry where the Rev. Trevor Dearing and I set her free from the spirits controlling her. When she was herself again, she confessed to being involved in witchcraft when she was younger.

48

Many years later the woman wrote to me. Apparently a friend reminded her of that night and told her exactly what she had said. She was shocked and apologised profusely. Curious how people react to swearing. Often it is the more expressive Anglo-Saxon counterpart of a dull Latin-based word. Sadly the growing middle-class find these words socially unacceptable.

As there were only a handful of us working in this field, I became an 'expert' who they called on to give an opinion. One of the recurring questions was 'What words do you use when exorcising evil spirits?' Strange how we always look for formulas. As I never found any particular words or phrases worked, I was at a loss to give an answer. One time I turned the question around on a particularly pushy reporter.

'What words do you use to get rid of a door-to-door salesman', I said. 'I don't know,' said the reporter from the Evening Standard. 'But you would make quite sure he left, wouldn't you?' I said. 'Well, that's all I do. I make sure it leaves', His report in the paper ended with these words: 'The Rev. George Tarleton said that expelling demons was like kicking out a door-to-door salesman'. One of these brave sales people later wrote to me. He said his job was difficult enough without being thought of as the devil.

The bishop of Exeter set up a study group on exorcism to which I was invited. They were also very interested in formulas. As the majority were Anglicans, they were set on finding some common ritual. My simplistic approach did not help - what did they expect from a nonconformist. Strangely enough it was very difficult to find any common ground. Opinions ranged from a psychiatrist who said mass for the dead to the Hampstead vicar who invited the demons into his own body. Seeing him perform on TV, shaking from head to toe, I felt my approach was safer.

Although this eclectic bunch were unable to agree about anything, later groups must have been more successful as they have now appointed an exorcist in every diocese. Once again this is a difficult area to prove exists, as the police are finding out in cases of the ritual abuse of children. But, as Hamlet said to his friend when talking about his father's ghost, 'There are more things in heaven and earth, Horatio, than are dreamt of in your philosophy.'

Unlike healing, exorcism turned out to be more successful. The success rate was nearer to 90 per cent. Whereas healing (or rather the lack of it) drove me to despair; this ministry produced an elation which was hard to handle. You start seeing demons round every corner. It becomes difficult to sort out the difference between a purely psychological problem and a demonic one. Casting out imaginary spirits becomes easier than dealing with a damaged human spirit.

After appearing on radio and TV, I became known as the ouija trouble -shooter. Various Christian teachers began asking me to speak in their schools and colleges on the dangers of dabbling in the occult. Christian Union meetings were always packed. Eventually it dawned on me that my denouncing the occult made it all the more fascinating. Feeling I was doing more harm than good, I stopped.

Before that moment arrived, I was asked to take a seminar on the occult at a convention called 'Spree 73'. This 'spectacular' was sponsored by the Billy Graham organisation, with the great man himself at the centre. As part of his team, I was granted a few minutes with Mr. Graham and Dorothy met him too. She had gone forward at one of his crusades in the 1950s and was over the moon when she met him. She did not wash her hand for days.

As he was thinking about writing a book on the occult, we used the subject to sound each other out. What impressed me most was the sense that here was a man in whom there was no guile. This was heightened by the religious mafia who surrounded him. Although his simplistic message no longer appeals to me, I still feel privileged to have met someone who could be truly called a man of God.

Deciding to cash in on my good luck, I published my first book the 'The Occult Mushroom'. This sold very well as each seminar had well over a thousand people. But soon after this event the company publishing my book went out of business. A couple of years later I put it with another publisher. They also went bankrupt. At the time I felt the devil was stopping the truth getting out but now I realise that, if any supernatural agency was involved, it was the good guys saving me from blushing in later years.

50

Dorothy in her wisdom, warned me about not being so dogmatic in the book. But when you are a fundamentalist that is like asking the dog not to bark. Believing that I was dealing with a cancer in society, I took a swipe at anything vaguely occult - even things like homeopathy and acupuncture.

The word 'occult' comes from the Latin *occultus*' meaning secret or hidden. Strictly speaking Jesus' teaching was sometimes occult. He said he spoke in parables so that his teaching would be hidden from the wise and prudent and understood by babes. Some early Christians believed that the heart of Jesus message was secret. Valentinus claimed that Paul taught this 'secret wisdom' only to those who were ready for it. There is a hint of this in the apostle's first letter to the Corinthians.

Ignorant of these things at the time, and ignoring my wife's counsel, I went ahead and published. The result was typically evangelical, even though the Evangelicals themselves had ignored demonology. While I still believe that Satanism and black magic are to be avoided like the plague, many of the things I denounced were harmless. Like most fundamentalists I had an irrational fear of anything I did not understand. At the time I was unaware that I was about to find a fundamental flaw in fundamentalism.

JUMPING SHIP

Meanwhile back at the local church a storm was brewing. Not because of my praying for the sick or casting out demons. Most of this went on behind closed doors - except once when I was baptising a young girl.

Baptists, as their name implies, differ from the other mainline churches on the mechanics of baptism. Immersion, they say, is the only way. The others believe that children can be initiated into the church when they are infants. Ducking babies under the water seemed a bit drastic, so the others opted for sprinkling. Baptists also feel that you cannot renounce the world, the flesh and the devil by proxy. Most 'godparents' have not done it for themselves, so how can they do it on behalf of the child?

At college I decided the Baptists had a point. Arguing my case from the Bible, I set out to convince my local church that baptism was an adults-only practice. To argue the case for children you need a degree in theology, so I won easily. The Baptist church was delighted to loan us their baptistry. However they were a bit taken aback by what happened.

The first person I baptised was Bruce. We became friends at college and he was now the minister of a Congregational church. When I had finished baptising everyone, he came back and baptised me. Thrown by this unorthodox approach, the Baptists asked me to explain. Answering one question with another I said, 'Who baptised John the Baptist?' Unable to answer, they went away muttering to themselves.

On the next occasion, I was thrown by what happened. Another Congregational church asked me to immerse a handful of their people. Half way through the service, the girl I was about to immerse began screaming her head off. Initially I thought she was afraid of water, but her husband assured me she was not. Realising we were not dealing with a rational problem here, I began to probe. When we discovered she had been mixed up in witchcraft, I took her out into the vestry.

This turned out to be one of those rowdy affairs with blood-curdling screams. I was not too worried about this since I had presumed the congregation would be led in a bit of hymn singing while I was dealing with the girl. When I took her back to the pool, I discovered the congregation had heard everything as they were asked to pray silently. After this, I thought it would be the last baptism I would conduct.

How wrong I was. Seeing the calm way in which the girl re-entered the pool, smiling radiantly, many felt they were missing something. We had to re-book the baptistry immediately as many waverers were now convinced there was more to baptism than just getting wet.

The storm clouds that were gathering had nothing to do with these strange goings on. It was more to do with mundane things like changing from the blue hymnbook to the red, spontaneous singing at the 'Lord's table', young people calling the minister by his Christian name etc. Rather than squabble about the minutiae, I decided to bring my hidden agenda out into the open and lift the discussion to a higher plane.

As my first five years were coming to an end, it seemed fitting to point to where the next five could lead to. In a nicely printed leaflet, I outlined the way forward. First, the church needed to become more of a community. Secondly, we needed to explore the whole area of worship without having to look over our shoulder. Lastly we needed to experiment with the gifts of the Spirit more openly.

Coming out of my charismatic closet, I knew I was about to lose my reputation for being a 'balanced young man'. But as the Master I followed 'made himself of no reputation', I decided to follow suit. Testing the waters, I was amazed that two thirds of the church were in favour of change. This was the majority required to carry anything through in the church meeting, the policy making body.

But the minority worried me. Although angry at their stubborn refusal to join in what God was obviously doing, I also felt great sympathy for them. Many had given their money, time and energy to keep this church going. Their social life revolved around this assembly. Despite praying for the church to be filled, the answered prayer didn't match their expectations. The choir was disbanded. Worship seemed so foreign. Age counted for very little. Familiar landmarks were disappearing. Somehow it seemed heartless to drag them screaming into this new kingdom. 'Thus conscience does make cowards of us all'.

Looking for a way out, I bumped into John Noble. He started life in the Salvation Army. Although he was no longer part of the organisation, no one could separate him from his trumpet. He had started meeting with a few friends in his home and began experimenting with all the things I had outlined in my printed pamphlet. My admiration for him at that time was great. So when he pressed a piece of paper into my hand saying 'I believe God wants me to give this to you', I could hardly wait to open it.

'You are like a captain standing at the helm of a ship', it said. 'Your leaflet has been like an order to cast off. While the crew have been happy to talk about the destination, they are frightened of the wind that will carry them there. Even if they are willing to set sail, there is a problem. The ship isn't a real ship, it's just a training ship. It cannot go anywhere as it has a cement bottom'.

Initially I laughed, then the message sank in. Now my internal reluctance to push through the changes I saw as vital, became clear. There was no point - we were not going anywhere. Putting to sea in a cement-bottomed ship put people's lives at risk. It was absurd to try. At that moment I knew I had to resign my leadership, there was no alternative.

My resignation was a bombshell and I was thrown by my own reaction. I retired to my vestry to let it sink in. As I closed the door, I burst into tears. Emotions that had been held in, now burst past the self-imposed dam. My body convulsed as the shock of what I had done hit me. What had seemed so clear-cut moments before, now looked distorted by my grief.

Why was I leaving what others called a successful church? Had not the numbers doubled and the offerings trebled? Was not the church filled with vibrant young people? What would happen to them now? Where did I go from here? Questions flooded into my overactive mind, but no answers.

The church had been the other woman in my life. Seven days a week were devoted to her, often at the expense of my family. Dorothy rarely complained. She just made up for my lack of what is now called 'quality time' with the children. Ending my affair with the Congregational Church in South Chingford turned out to be a very painful process.

Numbed by the effect of my decision, I decided to take up the many invitations to preach around the country.

Again I failed to see that I had left Dorothy holding the baby. Not only did she have to look after the kids, she also had to try to explain my disappearance. Many people called at the manse, stunned by my decision, and she was left to pick up the pieces. Often she would walk the dog in the park weeping her heart out, feeling I had let her down. I had, but was blissfully unaware of it until much later.

Being a realist, she was concerned about where we would live. The church had generously allowed us to stay on in their manse for three months. Dorothy knew the time would fly by. When she challenged me, I glibly replied that God would provide. Strangely enough he did. Hundreds of pounds began to turn up in my bank account. To this day I do not know the names of the people who did this wonderful thing. It was enough to put a deposit on a house and throw my tax inspector into a quandary.

During this time, one of the invitations I took up was to preach in Sweden with John Noble. We used it as a springboard to smuggle Bibles behind the Iron Curtain. As our time in Sweden had been hectic, we forgot to hide the Bibles. The two large cardboard boxes on the back seat stood out like a couple of pensioners at a disco. Glasnost was twenty years away.

Approaching the border, a surly guard demanded to see our documents. Casting a suspicious eye over us, he pointed to the car's registration number. 'This your number?' We nodded timidly. Walking round to the front, he checked it out for himself and began laughing. Pointing to the letters he said, 'In my country this means cat!' For some strange reason he found it funny. John and I made a pathetic attempt at laughing, as we were not looking forward to the next bit. Each car was methodically searched for at least five minutes. But the guard just waved us on, without looking in. Once out of sight we laughed our heads off.

After risking our lives to get the Bibles behind the Iron Curtain, the local Christians were more interested in us. The fact that their brothers in the West had not forgotten them was of more value than the Bibles.

Fellowship was more precious than books, even holy books. Living in dangerous situations can sometimes give you a better sense of priorities.

I did one more trip and decided I was not cut out to be a smuggler. Although it was exciting stuff, I thought it best to leave it to those who had a real burden for taking the Bible to countries where it was banned. I wanted to explore this mysterious thing called fellowship. Dissatisfied with my experience of modern Christianity, I set out on a search for a simpler, purer expression of my faith.

Surely it was pure when it began. What was it like when it was new and unspoiled by dogma? Setting out to discover the golden age of Christianity, I was forced to search the source documents for answers. Dr. Luke described the birth of the church succinctly. 'They met constantly to hear the apostles teach, and to share the common life, to break bread, and to pray. A sense of awe was everywhere, and many marvels and signs were brought about by the apostles. All whose faith had drawn them together held everything in common...' (Acts 2. NEB.) In other versions the words 'to share the common life' is translated as 'fellowship'.

CHURCH IN THE HOUSE

The Charismatic Movement gave birth to an anarchic animal. Injecting an adventurous spirit into traditionalists like me, it made us want to experiment. On returning from my preaching tour, I found a ready-made laboratory. About twenty people followed me out of the local church, leaving it more or less intact.

Meeting in someone's front room seemed the obvious thing to do. Ted and Peggy Rogers jumped at the idea of using their large front lounge. They felt their gift was hospitality. Little did we realise we were in at the start of the 'house church movement'. This was later to develop into what the media now calls the 'new churches', because we moved away from the early simplicity of the church in the house. Now some of the pioneers are spending thousands of pounds buying old church buildings or building new ones.

By comparison the church in the house is a very cost effective way of running a church. No time or energy is squandered on repairing or renewing old buildings. Money seems to be poured into a bag with holes in trying to keep these tottering edifices from decay. When people like Ted and Peggy were longing to have their homes used, building new structures seems such a waste of resources.

The main feature of these early house churches was a sense of freedom. It was thrilling being set free from the dead formalism that was squeezing the life out of Christianity. Our emphasis was on experience, relationships and free expression in worship. Sometimes this worship was silent, sometimes it was noisy. Some even dared to dance. This 'joy hop' was not a pretty sight. You were more impressed by the effort involved than the grace, but it was full of life. New vitality gave birth to new songs, set to music the young could relate to.

At our meetings there was a sense that anything could happen because there was no overt leadership. Those of us who did take a lead were always encouraging others to chip in. Initially few did. Being used to a one-man-ministry, it seemed strange now to take part. Although we had come out of the institution we call the church, it took years to get the institution out of us. I began to realise why St. Paul could be so free one minute and take a Jewish vow the next. Unfortunately he brought his

Jewish religion with him and shackled us to its guilt for nearly two millennia.

One of our young women invited her mum to come along to one of our meetings. Naively we thought she would be really impressed but half way through she walked out. When asked why she did this her comment was 'It was like watching two people make love, I felt like a voyeur'. What we had forgotten was how bizarre these free-wheeling, flexible gatherings appeared to the outsider. Having now watched these meetings through the cold eye of television, I now feel that worship is not for the public gaze. Like sex, it is too intimate for non-participants to appreciate.

Peter Hill had popped into one or two of those early meetings. On returning home from India, after a few years as a missionary, he was genuinely shocked to find Britain in the grip of the 'permissive society'. Although rather naive, Peter was used as a rallying point to gather a most unusual cross-section of Christendom. Under the banner 'Against Moral Pollution', he gathered Catholics and Evangelicals, religious establishment figures and the anarchic house churches.

Malcolm Muggeridge was one of those establishment figures Peter approached. He agreed to join if they changed the negative war cry Against Moral Pollution to the more positive 'Festival of Light'. Muggeridge always appeared anarchic, especially when he was debunking establishment figures and institutions. But after he saw the light and turned to Christianity, he became less critical of its practices.

One example of this is a debate we had about the Lord's Prayer. We were both being interviewed at a large rally at the Royal Albert Hall. As a journalist, he said the Lord's Prayer was the most concise piece of prose ever written. So he had no difficulty repeating it like a parrot twice a day as an expression of his love. I argued for a more spontaneous expression of love, saying my wife would become bored with the same form of words used morning and evening. Those who watched the debate were divided about who 'won'.

Privately we also discussed the place of law. What surprised me was his conservative views on law and order. He thought my ideas were anarchic. Rather like a Marxist, he was radical when looking in from the outside, but authoritarian when on the inside. His freedom needed form. It was no surprise when Malcolm entered the Roman Catholic church later in his life. Looking back I can now see why he joined in the Festival of Light -- it was the embodiment of right-wing Christianity.

The rally in Trafalgar Square on Saturday 25th September 1971 was massive to me. Never having been to a football match, I had never experienced anything as partisan as this. As one of the officials at the back of the platform, I was overwhelmed at the sight of so many Christians gathered in one place. As a large proportion of the crowd were from the new house churches, there was a lot of singing and dancing.

But apart from these spontaneous outbursts of praise, the Festival of Light never quite lived up to its name. All the speakers were against moral pollution, rather than for the Light. Some were very boring. The following day I marched into their headquarters in Woodford, saying they had accomplished their task and should shut up shop. They agreed, but carried on until it fizzled out a few years later.

During the Festival of Light, many of the members in the new house churches found out how many of us there were. 'Group leaders had been telling them of an emerging movement of the Spirit, now they could see for themselves,' says Dr. Andrew Walker. 'The Festival of Light did not give birth to Restoration, but it did confirm that 'something' was emerging. That something was still essentially an anarchic animal.' His book, *Restoring the Kingdom,* is a most accurate account of the birth of these new churches.

Clusters of these new churches began to come together for communal worship. These gatherings were not confined to those who shared the same doctrines, although they were all loosely evangelical. The thrill of finding other groups all over the country with similar origins, drew us together. Out of these times a common vision was born. We dreamt of being united by a variety of relationships, instead of being divided by dogma.

To begin to make the dream a reality, a handful of us began to call the representatives from these house churches in and around London together. The handful of hopefuls was Gerald Coates, David Mansell,

John Noble, Maurice Smith and myself. This core group became known as the 'London Brothers', although I was the only one who lived in London.

It would be difficult to imagine a more eclectic bunch of men. Gerald Coates was a great front man who was unafraid to show his emotions publicly. David Mansell was brash and awkward, but his insight and sense of the ridiculous were vital to us. Maurice Smith was a brilliant raconteur whose stories, like good wine, improved with age. His nervous weakness was his strength, unlike John Noble with his rock-like character. Although this sometimes turned out to be stubbornness, John's ability to draw things together was essential.

As it is difficult to see yourself as others see you, here is what Andrew Walker says of yours truly. 'George Tarleton was always the odd man out. His politics and theology were anarchic, and his general views more liberal than his colleagues.' Being the odd one out in this odd grouping of outlaws was no problem. No respectable Christian would have anything to do with us. We were *persona non grata*.

Appropriately the Leprosy Mission in London was chosen as the first venue of this meeting of outcasts. Nobody led the meeting formally, free expression was the norm. The idea of leadership was against our do-your-own-thing ethos. Initially I found it a little unnerving, especially the volume of praise. How could thirty to forty men make such a row? Noise and the gradual increase of numbers forced the owners of the room to ask us to find another meeting place. They were worried the ceiling would fall down.

By the time our numbers had reached 500, we had moved to the London School of Economics. During the early seventies the LSE was a focus of radical activity. But any student putting their head round the door of the lecture hall would not have been impressed with this strange gathering. However, within the context of the Christian church, we were radical.

When the numbers reached 1000, Maurice Smith suggested we hire the Friends Meeting House in London. Once again the name seemed fitting. From the start, John Noble had insisted that friendship should be the foundation on which we built. The quality of friendship we had in mind is summed up in that old Arab proverb. 'A friend is one to whom one may pour out all the contents of one's heart – chaff and grain together – knowing the gentlest of hands will take it and sift it, keep what is worth keeping and, with a breath of kindness, blow the rest away.' John became one of the best friends I ever had.

One of the recurring phrases during those formative days was 'You are not hearing me'. We had to learn to listen to each other with a new openness. Listening is difficult. Most of the time we are either agreeing or disagreeing with the person speaking, rather than listening. One of the most important discoveries I made was that communication only occurs when there is a sense of communion. Whether you agree or disagree is unimportant. Only when there is a sense of equality can we explore things together.

Maurice Smith, who always seemed more open to the promptings of the Spirit, suggested we should hire the Royal Albert Hall as our next venue. Until that moment the meetings had grown by word of mouth. This time we felt there should be some sort of advert. So half a dozen of us put our first names on a hand written leaflet. 'Come and praise God together at the Royal Albert Hall with Dave, George, Gerald, John, Maurice and Nick.' Nick Butterworth's inclusion into the core group of the London Brothers was a breath of fresh air. He was creative in a contagious way.

Looking back, this audacious call to worship in a vast auditorium in the centre of the capital was courageous. Organised groups had only managed to fill the place with expert help. Our casual, off-hand approach could have landed us with nothing but a large bill for hiring the hall. Yet somehow the 6000 seats of the Albert Hall were filled with exuberant, joy-filled worshippers from all denominations. 9000 actually turned up! There was a great sense of oneness that night, despite all our doctrinal differences. So much so that I felt moved to speak out against what I called 'the abomination of denominations' which kept God's people apart. In the excitement of that night, you could see all the man-made barriers tumbling down. Unfortunately they did not.

Leaders began to suspect we were starting yet another denomination. Nothing could have been further from our minds. John Noble's booklet 'Forgive Us Our Denominations', caught the spirit of our movement. Although we never said people should come out of their dead churches, many leaders saw it was implicit in where we were heading. After another couple of Royal Albert Hall meetings, we once again found ourselves outside mainstream Christianity.

When the irresistible force of the Spirit meets the immovable object of the Institution something had to give. Having tasted some of the new wine of the Spirit, it was too late to tell them about the dangers of alcohol. Jesus predicted that the new wine which God ferments would split inflexible wineskins. It did. There was an eruption of small groups meeting in people's homes.

LIBERATING WINE

My own path from hidebound evangelical to connoisseur of this liberating wine was slow and painful. In the midst of all this action it is important to remember I was a reactionary to start with.

One example of my reactionary nature is seen in my attempts to close down a local cinema. It was to be the first porn cinema to be sited outside the red light district of Soho in London. At the time I was still a respectable minister of a recognisable church. Joining together with other churches, we got thousands of people to sign our petition asking the government to ban the development.

Patrick McNair Wilson, our local Tory MP, jumped at the opportunity to help us present the petition to the Home Office. Any kind of publicity helps when you are on the opposition benches. At the Home Office, we were ushered into Shirley Williams' chambers. Being apolitical I did not realise she was one of the rising stars in the political arena. But I do remember she was far more impressive than the patronising politician presenting our case. Although she was very intelligent, she was still a good listener. However she was powerless to help.

Like a lot of moral campaigners, I had never actually seen what I was trying to ban. Had I done so, I would have realised that the lack of passion and poor quality of the porno movies would have bored their clients to death. That is precisely what happened. After a few years the cinema closed because of lack of interest.

Ordinary films can be far more erotic. But because my workload as a minister was so time-consuming, I rarely darkened the doors of a cinema. Then one day I was invited to preview the film 'Don't Look Now'. Billed as an occult thriller, the makers wanted to see what Denis Wheatley and other experts on the occult thought of it. Directed by Nicolas Roeg, the film took you into a world where you could not be sure what was real and what was illusion. The occult content was so brilliantly done that it could not offend.

What did shock me was my own reaction to one particular scene. While waiting in their hotel room in Venice, the husband and wife made love. They gave the cameraman an Oscar for the beautiful way in which this scene was shot. It was so realistic. Perhaps it was due to the fact that Julie Christie and Donald Sutherland were having an affair at the time.

Up to that moment, all that I had ever seen on screen was the occasional breast or two. What stunned me was how stimulating it all was. Enjoying the scene made me feel like a naughty schoolboy. Fearing my comments might make the headlines, I slipped out before the lights came on. Either my morals were questionable or I needed to question my moral code. I took the cowards way out and blamed myself for what was a normal, red-blooded male response. Deep within there were questions which would one day surface.

Questions came thick and fast as I counselled people. Initially it was simple. Black was black and white was white. There were no greys. Like my friend Eddie said: 'Abortion is never right'. Eddie had seven children. Deciding to play devil's advocate I said, 'Suppose your wife was pregnant and the doctors said she wouldn't survive childbirth, would you consider termination?' 'Never', he said without a moments hesitation. 'But your wife would die, Eddie', I protested. 'She would go to heaven', he countered. 'What about the children?' 'If we obey God's law that is His responsibility', was his trite reply.

Even though we were discussing it theoretically, I found myself deeply disturbed. Taking the life of any living being has always repelled me. Killing a half-dead gerbil almost proved too much for me. Soon after my chat with Eddie, I was faced with the real thing. Abortion is not an issue you can avoid when you become involved in other people's lives.

Sally was a very religious soul. During her pregnancy the doctors discovered she had a serious heart condition. 'Your heart cannot take the strain of giving birth to another child', she was told. Even though her doctor was a Roman Catholic, he suggested she should have an abortion. Unable to come to terms with his advice, she turned to me. Initially her husband was all for leaving it to God to sort out. But as we prayed and talked it through, it became clear that the doctor was right. Decisions like this are never easy and always distressing. Life is far more complicated than our simple moral codes.

Some people say you should follow your conscience. To many, conscience is the voice of God. For me the word has become soiled by its association with guilt. When we speak of having something on our conscience, we mean we feel guilty about it. How do you separate conscience from conditioning? To me it appears that the myriad voices of family and friends, pedagogues and peers combine in weaving together the set of rules we live by. Once we begin to question the basis of why we feel guilty, we are on the road to freedom.

Religion is the basis of most people's guilt, even though they are no longer religious. God does not set any standards. Religions do. They claim them to be God's on the basis of some holy book. Obey them and He will bless you, disobey and He will curse you. God's judgement is conveniently delayed until the next life, so there is no way of testing the thesis.

The first God-given law we challenged was the easiest to contest. The command to keep one day of the week holy when the whole week should be His, seemed a contradiction to us. Every religion has its holy day. Friday to the Muslim, Saturday to the Jew, Sunday to the Christian. This last one is the dodgiest of them all, covering up a crafty switch which took place during the reign of Constantine.

The Emperor, who converted Christianity to his cause, never stopped worshipping the sun-god. Like all soldiers he was superstitious, the more gods he had on his side the better. For him there was no difference between God the Father and Mithras, the sun-god. His edict to cease trading on 'the great and venerable day of the sun' is still being obeyed in many Western nations. Many believe the fable that the early Christians decided to change the Sabbath from Saturday to Sunday as it was the day their Lord rose from the dead. The truth is that it was changed on the whim of a dictator who was hedging his bets with the gods.

Knowing all this helped a little on the first Sunday we decided not to meet. Yet I still felt as if I were playing truant, especially when the sacred hours of ll a.m. and 6.30 p.m. approached. When guilt reared its ugly head, I reminded myself that Jesus was a sabbath-breaker. Until then Sundays were the busiest day of my hectic week. Suddenly here was a day to do with as I pleased. Sayings like 'The sabbath was made for man and not man for the sabbath', began to make sense.

Only those who have been caught up in the ritual can fully appreciate the relief we felt. After a while we wondered what all the fuss was about. Challenging the unwritten rules caused a greater stir. We began going to the theatre, having a meal out, drinking wine, going to the pub for a pint, dancing at discos etc. All innocuous enough, unless you come from a strict religious background. Any whiff of pleasure and it was deemed to be sinful by the evangelicals. So we were branded as gluttons and drunkards as Jesus was.

Counselling hundreds of people was only one reason for seeing that morals were never absolute. The other was the Bible. In those days I would never do anything which could not be justified within its pages. Reading through Paul's letter to the Galatians, I saw that those who learned to live by the spirit within were no longer subject to external codes. Coming from his fanatically Jewish background, Paul had greater problems with this than I did. His letter to the Romans shows how he wrestled with this, the seventh chapter in particular. 'We are discharged from the law to serve God in a new way', was his verdict, 'the way of the spirit, in contrast to the old way, the way of a written code'.

Pushing away all the props (which make us feel secure) is scary. But real learning only occurs when you do away with all external authority and turn to the light within ourselves. It is a frightening place to be as there is nothing to hold on to. The challenge is to accept that there are no absolutes but God.

Without the law would not anarchy and chaos reign? Because there is something frightening about the word 'anarchy', we tend to want to bury it. But most of us have an anarchic streak somewhere within. A recent MORI poll showed people trusted doctors most. Bottom place was reserved for government ministers. 'To be governed is to be noted, registered, controlled, taxed, drilled, held to ransom, exploited, monopolised, extorted, squeezed, hoaxed and robbed'. Although that statement was written by the anarchist Proudhon in 1851, it is even more relevant in a world of computerised information.

Anarchy rarely gets a good press. The events in Eastern Europe at the end of 1989 were anarchic. News programmes became riveting as we watched Germans, Czechs and Romanians revolt against their leaders with breath-taking speed. For me the most lasting image is of the crowd pouring over the Berlin Wall, some trying to demolish it with their bare hands. The media called this anarchy 'people power'.

What made these events unusual was the corporate anarchy. It is the individual who is anarchic. Our corporate experience is that we easily follow leaders, even corrupt ones. Having good rulers is no safeguard. Karl Marx said we should let the workers rule because they would rule on the behalf of the great mass of society. Bakunin, Marx's great rival, said we should not have any rulers at all. He argued that if you make workers rulers, they cease to be workers and become rulers. As such they would not follow the interests of the workers but the interests of the rulers. The historical process has proved the Russian anarchist right, and Marx wrong.

Surely you cannot be a Christian and an anarchist? Why not? The founder of Christianity was. Christ always had problems with leaders, partly because he seemed to like putting them down with one-liners. 'Render to Caesar the things that are Caesar's and to God the things that are God's' was a good one. And partly because they knew where his anarchic spirit would lead. Kicking the money-changers out of the temple may seem insignificant in our secular society. The modern equivalent would be putting a 'virus' into all the computers in the Stock Exchange. 'It's more to your interest that one man should die for the people, than that the whole nation should be destroyed', said the leader of the nation. So Jesus was executed in the national interest. He is a threat to any nation which puts the state before the individual, whatever the colour of its politics.

ANARCHY BRIDLED

While we were drawing large numbers of people together across the denominational spectrum, a man called Jimmy Owens was creating something new. Burdened by the lack of unity among God's people, he decided to try to draw them together. Being a composer, he used his musical gift. It took many months to complete his unique creation. In the process he had to sell his most precious possession - his piano - in order to feed his family.

The musical presentation he composed was fittingly called 'Come Together'. Musically it ranged somewhere between rock and easy listening. Its hook line was 'Come together in Jesus' name'. The message seemed tailor-made for our situation. At first John Noble did not seem too keen, partly because the initial London presentation was narrated by the singer Pat Boone. How could we follow that?

After a while I managed to badger him into allowing his fellowship to join with ours in taking the musical around London. Together these groups formed the choir which lay at the heart of this show.   Audience participation also played a major part in this charismatic event. People were encouraged to pray for each other in specific ways. I was always embarrassed by this and managed to excuse myself as I had been narrating.

It proved such a success that we took over the Rainbow Theatre in Finsbury Park for one evening. This theatre had been the exclusive domain of rock stars. Yet here was a group of nobodies filling the place. Caught up in the joy of the event, I began to dance. Even Pat Boone did not do that. Many people were enriched by this multi-media approach. But the greatest impact was on those of us involved in the show.

On the final performance Bob Gillman, one of the local songsmiths, asked if he could sing something to the choir. 'Bind us Together' was the song he had just composed and it seemed to capture the spirit of what was happening among us. But it was too good for just a backstage performance, so I built it into the programme. Now it is sung around the world and Bob regularly receives the royalties for it. Ironically he is no longer in one of the new churches, because we changed something spontaneous into a new set of rules and it became a bind in the wrong sense.

It all started when we began to realise that we were riding an anarchic animal. Anything could happen. All our options were open. We could go anywhere, do anything. But as 'leaders' we felt we had to act responsibly. Responsibility is a curious word. Normally we use it to indicate a sense of duty, of doing the right thing. But it also means having the ability to respond to new situations in creative ways. Regrettably we felt the need to do the 'right' thing, but no one seemed to know what that was.

Almost as an answer to our unspoken prayer, we were introduced to some leaders from Argentina. They had been working with a well known man called Juan Carlos Ortiz and claimed to have the answer to our God-given chaos. As Argentina was experiencing the same spontaneous movement of the Spirit, we felt they could have found the next step.

The most charismatic of these South American preachers was Orville Swindoll. No prizes for guessing what we nicknamed him. 'Discipleship is the answer', he said. To those of us steeped in the New Testament, the word had an instant appeal. Jesus had disciples. He told them to go into all the world and make disciples of all men. 'It's simple', said Orville, 'All you have to do is to get your people committed and submitted to you.'

One of the Argentinians showed us the logistics of how to reach the world. We just had to disciple five men. They in turn would train five each making 25. If they took on five apiece, we would immediately have 125. These would swell the number to 625 with their five disciples. The next figure was mind boggling, they would raise the total to 3125 with their five disciples. What we did not realise was, it is a simple marketing technique. Networking, as it is called, has been around since the end of the war.

No sooner had they left, than the Americans came bearing a similar message. Unknown to us, they had also met up with Juan Carlos Ortiz and developed their own blend of this teaching. 'Shepherding is the answer', said Ern Baxter. He was the elder statesman of the Fort Lauderdale clan. When he spoke, it was spellbinding stuff: a strange mixture of gravity and humour. Jokes were delivered with a timing I have only seen with the comedian Victor Borge. As shepherding seemed very similar to discipling, we felt God must be saying something. 'Out of the mouth of two witnesses a thing is established', says the good book.

What we failed to realise was a division was beginning to creep in. Shepherds only had a function when there were sheep. Initially the London Brothers not only saw no difference between each other, we also looked on anyone coming to our meetings as friends. We despised the gap between clergy and laity. From the outset we saw ourselves as servants. 'The greatest among you must be your servant', Jesus said.

To make these new ideas acceptable to our free and easy folk, we repackaged them under the name of 'Commitment'. Now commitment is a beautiful thing when it is not forced. You only have to think of a young couple in love. To them commitment is no big deal. If you are a real friend to someone, commitment is built into the relationship. At the beginning our commitment had that flavour about it. But as soon as we started to spell out what we meant, something was lost. Commitment 'classes' now became necessary to sustain what had ceased to happen spontaneously.

Before pointing out the problems of going down this cul-de-sac, let me highlight some of the advantages to me. Our little church-in-the-house began to grow. Now there were two houses, we felt the need to get everyone together sometimes. So we hired the scout hut. Members from other small groups began to pop in to spy out our liberty. Some local groups decided to throw in their lot with us. Soon there was about two hundred of us meeting in the assembly hall of a local school.

Among our home-grown fellowship there was a handful of men who could give direction, if necessary. The groups who joined us came with their built-in leaders. These dozen men decided to commit themselves to me. Over the next few months our friendship grew. We called each other 'brother' and meant it. I had never known anything as close as this amongst men. Dorothy felt threatened by it. Whereas I used to open my heart to her about how I felt, now I did it within this new circle. She felt shut out.

Bob Finney was the man I was closest to. We had developed spiritually along similar lines. Also squash was an important part of our lives. There was no pressure when we got together. When I was invited to India to

70

preach for a few weeks, I took Bob with me. Missionaries were glad to hear his simple message: 'Know God for Himself'. Although he never felt at ease with my anarchy, he was big enough not to let it spoil something good.

At another level, I was invited to join with thirteen other men who travelled round the country preaching. We jokingly called ourselves the 'fabulous fourteen'. Getting together on a regular basis we would compare notes. Not knowing where I was going, it was good to meet with others who were searching for clues as well. Because we were all equal, we felt free to explore areas which we had not ventured into by ourselves. It was very stimulating.

After a few months it became clear that while we were all equal, some were more equal than others. Graham Perrins and Bryn Jones began to compete to be the first among equals. Both published rival magazines. 'Fullness' was the more radical of the two, but it bore the marks of Graham's roots in the Open Brethren. 'Restoration' had a wider appeal as it was closer to conventional Christianity. Bryn's classic Pentecostal background gave it an unmistakable flavour. I occasionally wrote articles for Graham's magazine, never for Bryn's.

Bryn Jones would have made it to the top of any business. Adept at manipulating people, he always made sure he got what he wanted. He not only had a clear vision, but the ruthless resolve to turn that vision into reality. If you wanted to be on the winning team, you would have joined Bryn's side. Unconsciously we were beginning to take sides.

When David Mansell, one of the London Brothers and one of the Fabulous Fourteen, moved into my area, I invited him to join me. After a few visits, he still felt on the outside, and asked to be 'officially recognised'. So we invited his friend Bryn Jones and my friend John Noble to speak at this awkward ceremony. Bryn had always viewed me with suspicion and John had never been comfortable with David. It felt like we were about to duel and these men were our seconds. There was to be a duel some time in the future, but for the moment Bryn said nice things about David and John said nice things about me.

Imagine my surprise when Bryn Jones started to prophesy about me. Our prophecy rarely contained a predictive element, but this did. First he said that I had been called to be an 'apostle', a strange term which I will explain later. Then he went on in his flowery Pentecostal way to explain that the Lord would show me why 'the green mountain of the Lord' would be burned black. In simple English this meant I would discover what ruined this growing work of God. I did. It was submission.

Submission was the unseen backbone of our new commitment concept. People had to submit themselves to God first, then to the leaders he placed over them. All this resulted in God's work being done with the minimum of fuss. I have to admit that, initially, it appealed to me. Things began to move. It looked as if we had bridled the anarchic animal and made it useful. But something died, because submission kills communication. Feedback was missing. Being an authority, or obeying, one cuts out real learning. Everything was now second hand. The green mountain was turning black.

Little things began to alert me to the problems we were producing. Let me give you a small example. The leader of another local house church was thinking of joining my expanding group of fellowships. 'My problem is your emphasis on submission', he said. 'You've got it all wrong', I countered. 'Take Roy (one of my leaders who happened to be standing next to me), if I asked him to mow my lawn at midnight, he would laugh in my face'. To my amazement, Roy was not so dismissive. 'If you asked me to do that I would, because I know you would have a a good reason for asking'.

My silly illustration had blown up in my face. I was speechless. Roy would mow my lawn at midnight simply because I asked him? What a mindless way to respond. Others were obviously taking it more seriously than I was. Perhaps I should. Why was I so reluctant to pull rank. Was it just a natural reticence? I was about to find out.

THE SIN OF SUBMISSION

Oblivious of the damage it would create, I began to implement this new concept of submission. Peter, another one of my leaders, fell under the spell of an American preacher, who was proclaiming himself to be a prophet. He began to collect a following among the house churches in and around London. Maurice Smith met the man and declared he was 'unclean'. Wanting to see for myself, I slipped into a meeting in the Tottenham fellowship.

His 'message' was simple. He was God's man for the hour. To prove it he knocked every other person who was being used in the Charismatic Movement -- even the London Brothers whom he had yet to meet. 'They say I am a dangerous man', said the American, 'Why haven't they bothered to check out what I am saying?' Little did he know I was at the back of the room. Cleverly using innuendo and insinuation, he ruined the reputation of everyone I had ever heard of. Within an hour of the onslaught, he was the only one whose integrity was still intact.

Peter fell for it hook, line and sinker. He was not normally a gullible man. Being a businessman he not only had a healthy scepticism, but also a strong desire to keep all his options open. On this occasion his critical faculties were put on hold. He demanded that we give this 'prophet' a platform within our newly grown church. Not wanting to expose it to the hot air of this overheated mind, I refused.

So Peter took it upon himself to ferry people to meetings where the American was spouting his spurious claims. Confronting Peter with his conspiracy only made it worse. After consulting many others it became clear that Peter must be 'put out of fellowship'. In other words, he must be kicked out of our house church. My life had been spent trying to get people into the church -- this was the only time I had ever shown anyone the door. But we could not tolerate this lack of submission.

On the night we were to put him out of fellowship, Peter did not turn up. I was glad as it took the steam out of the situation. I remember too there was an awful prophecy about what would happen to him if he did not repent from this persistent stubbornness. But after I explained to the church what had been going on, and our decision to expel Peter, Andy Milliken stood up. He thought this submission thing was very similar to the treatment he experienced in the war, especially under the Japanese. It was all too harsh. Unless we reversed our decision, he and his wife would be forced to leave. We could not, so they left. I was influencing people, but I was beginning to lose friends.

Andy was right, it was much too harsh. If only I had waited, there would have been no need for such drastic action. The American prophet was caught with his pants down, literally. While the men were at work, he was helping the women overcome their sexual frigidity. Another 'gift' God had apparently given him. Of course it was a hands-on approach which he used. When the leaders of the house-church found out about his activities, they packed his bags and put him on the next plane back to the States.

For a couple of years I heard nothing from Peter. Then he got word to me asking if we could meet. My immediate reaction was that he had seen the error of his ways. The sad truth was that he was dying of cancer and wanted to put his house in order. He asked me to forgive him. I asked him to forgive me. We gave each other a hug and I left. A great sadness descended on me as I drove home, a friendship had been ruined by demanding he should submit. What did it matter who was 'right' and who was 'wrong'? Surely friendship was enough. Peter died a few weeks later.

Submission spawned a new hierarchy. What took a century to emerge in the early church was springing up before our eyes within a decade. Bishops, priests and deacons were starting to rise above the rest. Church history was being repeated. We hardly noticed the change, it was so subtle. For a start we used different names. Deacons were called house group leaders. Priests were called 'elders' and were responsible for groups of people, most of the elders were young men. Few noticed the paradox.

The new bishops were called 'apostles' and 'prophets' as that was more biblical. Apostles were men who had founded (or were responsible for) some of these new churches that were springing up around the country. Prophets were men who felt they knew the direction these churches should be going in. Note the absence of women in all this. As they were to be in submission to their husbands, it was difficult for us to see how a man could submit to a woman.

The end of a meeting of elders in Belfast illustrates this. During discussion, I admitted that I often submitted to my wife as her intuition had so often proved to be right. Everyone was about to go home when I made this casual remark. The meeting went on for a further two hours as they tried to show me how wrong I was. They argued that when Dorothy said something that was on the button, I judged it to be correct and submitted to my own judgement. Little did they know that I often judged what she said to be wrong and only time proved her right.

Submitting to Dorothy was unpalatable to them as I was an 'apostle'. This office died out a century after Jesus' death, as it became restricted to those who had witnessed his resurrection. As they died, so did this term. We resurrected it in the wider sense used by Paul. He called many people apostles who had not seen the risen Christ. Paul himself had only heard the risen Lord. But he was responsible for churches, hence his letters in the New Testament.

As I had planted the house church in my locality and was responsible for a few others, I was called an apostle. I must confess that when the term was first used of me, it triggered a frisson of delight. Later I started to play it down, saying it was what others called me. More recently, I appeared on a TV documentary, when the word 'ex-apostle' appeared under my talking head - I wanted to hide under the settee.

Being an authority reduces your ability to experiment. As you are supposed to know the answers, you avoid the awkward questions. Creativity goes into decline. Before this authority structure was in place, we were experimenting with worship. We never really knew where our meetings would end up. Once we booked the Albert Hall as an experiment. We called it an evening of Creative Praise. We sang, clapped, shouted and were silent. There was dance and drama. The whole area in front of the stage was a seething mass of moving humanity. Even the last night of the Proms was eclipsed by this emotional display of our love for the King of Kings.

When we began to learn obedience, a structure began to appear. Our creative juices began to dry up. Toward the end of my involvement with this movement, I became bored with these times of praise. They were just action replays of days gone by. The music lost its rough edge, the singing was more polished. We had become technicians of the Spirit. We knew how to turn 'it' on. The people had learned how to respond to our lead. We had boxed in the Spirit, everything became predictable.

Obviously some good things occurred when we learned to submit to one another. One time I turned up to a meeting with the London Brothers and almost fell asleep. They wanted to know why I was so shattered. When I explained that I was being called out at all hours of the day and night to deal with people who had been messing around with the occult, they said it must stop. As this one aspect of my ministry was beginning to take over my life, I was glad to submit to them. However, when we asked another member of the London Brothers not just to stop one facet of his work, but to stop speaking altogether - sparks began to fly.

Certain rumours began to surface about David Mansell's private life. As he was one of the 'London Brothers', we decided to confront him with them. Although he protested his innocence, we were not convinced. Also we asked him to drop out of circulation for a few months while the matter was cleared up. David refused to submit.

The content of the rumours was not the issue. To some extent we all felt 'there but for the grace of God go I'. The real problem was his attitude, it was appalling. David, telling us to get stuffed, threw this new submission teaching into clear focus. Leaders only obeyed when it suited them. It was convenient for me to submit to them, giving up my work with casualties from the occult world, as I was becoming a casualty myself. David did not submit as he felt his whole future was at stake.

Bryn Jones came to the rescue. David was his friend and he felt we were being too authoritarian. We were, but he was the last person who should have pointed it out. He ran such a tight ship in Bradford that the word 'mutiny' never crossed anyone's mind. Yet here he was taking our mutineer under his wing and scolding us for the way we handled this open revolt. Nevertheless we were glad that he was taking David off our hands.

What everyone seemed to forget was that David and I were still part of the same fellowship. Not just part of but joint leaders. I was the 'apostle' and he was the 'prophet' who was supposed to give direction to the church. Obviously I could not live with that, so I asked the dozen local leaders around to my house to discuss the problem. David was not invited.

My first shock was that David had decided to come anyway. He said nothing. But his brooding presence said it all. It was one of the most uncomfortable meetings I have ever attended. What is more, it was all happening under my roof. Undeterred, I pressed on. David's revolt obviously meant he had to stand down. Add to this, his submission to Bryn three hundred miles away, the matter seemed beyond question.

Alan Pavey, David's best friend, took on the mantle for counsel for the defence. What appeared so straightforward, now became complicated. Could the charges against David be proved? No, but that was not the issue. What was the issue? David's lack of submission. Was that not understandable with the way it was handled? Yes, but.... So it went on into the night. It ended in deadlock. Half were with me, half with David. I was stunned. 'We must take it to the church,' I said. 'No way' they cried. This time the elders were united. Their reason? The 'sheep' would not be able to cope with the problem. Leaders always patronise the led, we were no exception.

I agreed to abide by their decision. The matter was hushed up. To this day, the majority of the 300 members do not know the real reason for the church splitting in two. One minute we were singing 'Come Together', the next we were coming apart at the seams. Unable to tell half the church why they would never see me again, deeply grieved me. Today I would have ignored the leaders as David did. My cowardice meant that confusion reigned.

Losing my close friendship with half the leaders was numbing. Bob Finney was the man I missed most. At the time, his friendship with Alan Pavey was blossoming. Alan was a brilliant salesman. He was the managing director of Farah UK, a middle-of-the-road manufacturer of men's clothing. Now I can see how easy it was for Alan to turn Bob against me. At the time it felt like *Et tu, Brute*! I could not cope with his defection to David.

Recently, Bob and his wife Val came searching for us. They knew we were hiding out in the New Forest. Being a policeman, Bob managed to track us down. Admitting you are wrong takes courage, but he never lacked that. I was unable to hold back the tears, but too much water had flowed under the bridge to restore our original closeness. But it was good to laugh with him again.

Demanding submission was proving a costly business. Friendship, our initial goal, was going out of the door. So many people have been damaged by this pernicious teaching that most of the new churches have dropped the word. Commitment is now the password. So the wolf of submission is now passed off as a lamb. The walking wounded I have met over the past decade prove that the wolf has lost none of its teeth.

The problem for these walking wounded starts when they drop out of this high-octane blend of religion and spirituality. They feel they have tried the best form of Christianity and failed. Nothing could be further from the truth. Those of us who brought the doctrine of submission into the work of God are the failures. We failed to see where submitting would lead. Thinking it would build the kingdom of God, we found it just helped us build our own little kingdoms. Those who have the courage to walk out of these man-made kingdoms also feel that there is nowhere to go. One aim of this book is to prove there is 'life after fellowship'.

FLESHING OUT THE WORD

After a quarter of a century of studying the Bible and proclaiming it to be the Word of God, I found it was not. This revelation did not come from the dry academic writings of liberal thinkers, but from the pages of the New Testament itself. In the majestic opening verses of John's gospel, Jesus -- not the words of holy men -- is declared to be the Word. John was proclaiming the dawn of a new era. The Word was not to be written down but made flesh.

To underline this new way, Jesus quite deliberately chose not to leave behind anything written down by his own hand. Despite living among a people who set great store by the written word, there has never been a hint that Jesus might have left anything set down on paper. The Jewish religion had their words set in cold tablets of stone. This new faith was already written on the warm places of the heart -- the kingdom of God was already within, waiting to be discovered.

So when we are asked to ratify anything that Jesus is supposed to have said, we cannot. His words are lost in the elaborate web of invention and manipulation of the gospel writers. Yet somehow he manages to slip out of the religious garments of his age and confront us twenty centuries later. He is the combination of what we imagine and what we intuitively sense to be true. The man is the message: Jesus is the Word.

The enigmatic figure of Jesus continues to astonish, especially with his strange request that we should love our enemies. Nobody ever said that before. Few seem to understand it. Certainly not the modern fundamentalist prophets. Fuelled by the book of Revelation, they predict an apocalyptic end of man around the year 2000. Mankind's only hope, they say, is for Jesus to return and zap his enemies. Impossible. Jesus' way of destroying his enemy is to love him to death. He challenges us to believe that love will ultimately triumph.

Graham Perrins decided to publish my article, about the Bible not being the word of God, in his magazine 'Fullness'. Some found its message liberating, others found it threatening. Unknown to me, I had stumbled upon the fundamental flaw in fundamentalism. At the heart of all fundamentalism there is a book: the Koran, the Talmud, the Bible. Question the validity of that book and the system begins to collapse. At the time I was unaware of the far-reaching implications of my discovery. Others were and the word 'heretic' began to be bandied about.

About the same time I wrote another article called 'Joie de Vivre' suggesting we restore a healthy enjoyment of life to Christianity. Strangely enough this caused even more of a stir. To the religious, life was to be endured not enjoyed. Pleasure was a dirty word. Any exuberant enjoyment was to be postponed until we were on the other side of the grave. This jaundiced view of life seems the mark of being religious. It also marked a division within the 'Fabulous Fourteen'.

After Bryn Jones took David Mansell under his wing the cracks began to appear. Although we all agreed that we were free from the demands of living our lives by the rule book, to some it was merely a technicality. 'Although I am free to buy an ice-cream on a Sunday, I will not do it in case it causes my weaker brother to stumble.' Someone actually said that to me. Enshrined within that silly sentence is the double-think that makes religion dangerous. Freedom is given with one hand and taken away with the other. The touch of humility within it is a masterstroke.

Seven of the fourteen believed this 'weaker brother' clause virtually cancelled any freedom. The rest of us decided to explore our new-found liberty. Looking back it all seems so innocent. Take alcohol. Most of us drank it, but only half openly confessed to it. Some of us dressed in the latest fashions. Gerald Coates' clothes often bordered on the outrageous. Others looked as if they were bank managers. My half began to rekindle our love affair with the theatre. We also started seeing the latest films, regardless of what rating the censor had given them.

Funny how little things should cause big problems. The other half felt we were flaunting our liberty, we felt they were being hypocritical. Matters came to a head when the issue of masturbation, of all things, was raised. Gerald Coates and John Noble felt it was a natural act and the freedom-seekers agreed. Gerald wanted everyone to admit they masturbated sometimes. Ninety per cent of the room agreed they did. Half of us wanted to go public and declare it was not a sin, setting people free from unnecessary guilt. The rest were outraged.

To the outsider, this may seem trivial, but to those from a biblical culture, it was serious. Even though the Bible maintained a gentlemanly silence

80

on the subject, that did not stop the disciplinarians from insisting it was an unwritten law. Taking the text 'Touch not the unclean thing' completely out of context, they made it a pretext for avoiding this form of pleasure. Dire warnings about going blind was added to bolster their weak argument. (One boy asked if he could continue until he needed glasses!)

In hindsight, it is easy to see how the masturbation issue must have been the final straw to the more orthodox among us. We remained oblivious of the problems we were causing until the autumn of 1976. The London brothers (John, Gerald, Maurice and yours truly) decided to get together at Fairmile Court in Cobham. Gerald had discovered that this lovely country house on his doorstep could be rented for the day. We often retreated there from the noise of London when we wanted to sort things out. Although it was set in beautiful surroundings, its greatest asset was the squash court in the grounds.

The fact that we were joined by Graham Perrins, John MacLauchlin and Peter Lyne from the West Country should have alerted us to the unusual nature of this gathering. It did not. Then Graham read a letter from Arthur Wallis. We were stunned into silence. It was a bomb. Everything shattered. All that we had worked for lay in ruins. Seven preachers cannot remain silent for long. Regaining our composure, someone suggested it must be a joke. But Arthur never seemed to understand a joke, let alone think one up.

Arthur Wallis was chosen as chairman of the 'Fabulous Fourteen' as we all had a kind of respect for him. Son of a famous preacher, Captain Wallis, Arthur never really shed his Open Brethren persona. The Brethren, as their name implies, claim to have no leaders - but they do. This strange sect is known for its rigorous stance on the moral law. Arthur was no exception. Their 'law' went far beyond the ten commandments to include all the shibboleths of the evangelical wing of the church. Our flouting of the latter must have finally got under Arthur's skin.

His letter was, in effect, a list of the disagreements between the two factions of the 'Fabulous Fourteen'. Although there were a couple of references to theological issues, at the heart of the letter was a moral issue. He felt we were about to fall into licence. Part of the proof was that John Noble and I were 'associating with hairies'. You can see why we thought it was just a joke. Hairies was simply a name for people with long hair. John and I had been through a period of growing our hair long. What we saw as a passing fashion, Arthur saw as something more sinister.

Arthur ended his letter with his coup de grace: we were all deceived by the devil. Now this was Catch 22. If we agreed, we were condemned out of our own mouths. But if we claimed the charges were fatuous, as we did, that was taken as proof of our deception., After a lengthy discussion, someone tore up his copy of the letter. It seemed the only sane thing to do with it. Everyone else must have done the same as no copy exists of the edict today.

The immediate effect of this epistle was to split the movement in two. To be fair, Arthur is said to have regretted his weird pronouncements before he died. What a shame he never wrote to tell us. We were deeply hurt at the time. Thank God there was a squash court in the grounds. Our frustrations were taken out on the squash ball. Feeling we had to get away from all this madness, we took a break on the island of Majorca. Having our wives with us made it a fun time. If they were involved earlier, maybe none of this would have happened.

On our return, we got on with the building of what we thought was the kingdom of God. It had all the excitement of being a counter-culture, God's alternative society that was going to turn the world upside down. But somehow it never did. Perhaps because we were subconsciously trying to compete with those who had cut us off. We became the Christian entrepreneurs of the Eighties. Our numbers began to grow. Peddling our wares around the country, we offered our expertise under the name of 'covering'. Practically, that meant you submit your little fellowship to me, and you will be plugged into something greater.

Maintaining this 'greater something' demanded money, so tithing was re-introduced. Tithing -- giving one tenth of your income -- is a Jewish custom. All my warning bells began to ring. In the beginning there was no regular support for people like me. We 'lived by faith', relying on the Lord to prompt someone somewhere to send something. I admit it is a scary way of living, but it worked.

Some made it work by sending out 'prayer letters', which was just another name for begging letters. We did not. Earlier in this book I mentioned the mysterious way in which the deposit for my house came from 'nowhere'. But the everyday miracles of provision were just as exciting. Sometimes people even provided holidays for me and my family. Other times they would bring round some groceries. Mainly people just sent money in the post. It took some time for the tax man to rule what should be taxed and what should be called a 'gift'. The money we got from preaching was to be taxed, not the groceries on the doorstep.

Living by faith was replaced by tithing (except in the circles I was responsible for). They renamed it a 'Kingdom Principle'. Some said it was just a suggestion, but group pressure turned it into an obligation. Smelling a rat - one that dies in Old Testament times - I began to question where we were heading. All the indications were that we were going into reverse. The term 'restoration' has rightly been used by Dr. Andrew Walker to define the movement I was involved in. We felt we were restoring Christianity to an earlier time when everything was not just simpler but purer. Going back to the past was our future.

Len Moules confirmed my misgivings. Although not directly involved with the work we were doing, this great missionary had tried to keep a fatherly eye on us. Having been involved in tough uncompromising situations in places like Tibet, he knew how easy it was to lose your way. 'You guys are always on about recovering the purity of the early church', he said. 'This move of God is not about recovery but discovery'. That simple sentence opened up a whole new direction for me.

Later I was to discover that there never was a 'golden age' when Christianity was simpler and purer than its modern counterpart. Historically early Christianity contained an extraordinary range of viewpoints. Only a limited number of these views have been presented to us. From a strictly historical point of view, no single structure can ever claim to represent real Christianity. For the moment I was content to set out on the voyage of discovery Len had suggested. Some of these discoveries have changed for ever the way I view the world we live in.

THE MUSWELL HILL MOB

Dorothy was on the verge of a nervous breakdown. All the traumas of the last few years had caught up with her. For many months she had not been able to attend a meeting without bursting into tears. Being more gregarious than me, she missed the friends she made first in the church and later on in the fellowship. She tried to maintain friendships across the divisions that had occurred. The result was more pain.

Playing my 'role' as a man, I managed to hide my feelings for the moment. But I realised we had to move out of Chingford. Two options presented themselves. One was to become a part of a fellowship I was covering on the Isle of Wight, the other was to lead a house church in Muswell Hill. Moving to the Island was my choice as it was furthest away.

However, the London brothers said that they wanted me to stay in London, so we decided to go to Muswell Hill. The area was unique. It had become the overspill for the trendy, and now overpriced, Hampstead area. Attending a parents evening at the school, we found for the first time that English was not the dominant culture. We found it stimulating.

The fellowship was even more exciting. The bulk of them had been forced to leave the local Baptist church after experiencing being filled with the Spirit. It was a younger group, and as a result they were more flexible. Here was a group of Christians who were ready to experiment. Nothing was beyond question. Sacred cows could be sacrificed on the altar of our common experience.

Dave and Hilary Mellows led the group. Hilary was born in the area. After marrying, they became missionaries in Italy. Forced home because of family pressures and a lack of success, they became involved in the Charismatic movement. Their great forte was caring for people. They were a great help to Dorothy and, along with some of the others in the fellowship, gently nursed her back to her old self. Finally they took us on holiday to Italy, the land they loved.

Not only were Dave and Hilary caring, the whole fellowship was. Just being with them was therapeutic. Coming among them as one who was supposed to have all the answers, I soon learned they had more to teach me, especially about the place of women in the church. To my surprise, the wives of leaders attended leaders meetings too and had equal status with the men. Perhaps this was because Hilary was a very strong character. Some of the women were better at giving direction to the church than the men.

Sheila Sayers, for example, had a picture of us as a life-boat bobbing up and down on the sea. She said we were too isolated to affect those around us. So God was going to sink the boat so that it floated just below the surface. Although we would know who was in the boat, it wouldn't be obvious to those around us. This was the start of our getting involved with our neighbours - not to evangelise them, but just to be involved in the substance of their lives.

Next we started to involve single women in the leadership. Chris Batchelor was the first. She helped me re-think my attitude toward women taking the lead. Finally I arrived at the conclusion that no position of leadership should be exclusively male - not even being an apostle. To prove it to my peers, I had to back it up with some biblical proof. Delighted to find a couple of female apostles among Paul's epistles, I decided it was time to go public.

Kingdom Life, was a yearly event staged in the open air at Cobham in Surrey. Gerald Coates, one of the London brothers, organised the event. Christians from miles around flocked to the little town. One evening I held forth on my equal-opportunity-for-women revelation. Most women loved it. A few men did as well, but I was not invited to speak at Kingdom Life again.

Settling in with the Muswell Hill mob was easy. It was invigorating being in the midst of a people so open to change. Also, no one else could have coped with my family at that time. Laurie Young, one of the Muswell mob, was very helpful to us in this area. In his younger days he had been quite a tearaway himself. I first met him when he was a teenager and later when I was spiritual adviser to an evangelistic team he had joined. After a few years, when the team had served its purpose, I suggested they call it a day. Clive Calver went on to head up the Evangelical Alliance, Graham Kendrick to write more hymns than Charles Wesley, but Laurie outshone them all.

When it was first suggested that he should get a normal job, I did not feel he would get very far in the real world. He seemed a bit of a dreamer, not suited to the cut and thrust of big business. However, he joined British Telecom and swiftly rose to become its UK service marketing manager. As PA to the deputy chairman, he was intimately involved during its privatisation. From this launch pad, he has gone on to greater things including writing a book on customer care which has become a reference work.

Mark and Sharon were going through that awkward, rebellious phase when teenagers try to find their own identity. Hair is often the battleground. 'Dad, I am going to shave off all my hair and become a skinhead', said Sharon. 'No way!' I replied, gazing at her beautiful head of strawberry blonde hair. Threatening to take away her pocket money, her stereo and banning her from going out in the evenings only strengthened her resolve. We even said we would not take her on holiday with us. She did not budge. One day shortly after this, Dorothy and I were trundling home with bags of shopping. We found ourselves following a young lad who turned to go into our house. As he turned we recognised the face. Sharon! Stunned into action, I implemented all my threats.

Laurie Young, however, did not bat an eyelid when he saw her. Admiring what I found repulsive, he asked her what the two razor lines across her scalp were for. Before she had time to answer, I said, 'They are runways for fleas'. Sharon, who had not spoken to me for days, could not stop laughing. The cold war between us was over.

Mark went one better. Not only did he change his hairstyle, he also changed his lifestyle. Punk was a swear word at the time and he declared himself to be a punk. Sid Vicious was his idol. During my time as a 'normal' minister, I refused to wear a dog-collar. Now here was my son wearing a real dog-collar, spikes and all. Using boot polish to make his blonde hair black and spiky did not endear him to his mother.

One evening a young 'elder' from another part of the country came to speak to our Fellowship. Arriving at our house, he was filled with horror when introduced to Mark and Sharon. Having two small children of his own, he was anxious not to repeat our mistakes. 'Where do you think you went wrong with your children?' he solemnly asked Dorothy. Not too pleased with this line of questioning, she said that as far as she knew we had not done anything wrong.

'Why do you expect your children to conform to the status quo when you don't?' remarked Laurie to me one day. 'They take after you!' Laurie's perception about my kids stopped me in my tracks. I couldn't see any way in which they took after me whatsoever. But instead of being angry, I tried to understand the punk phenomenon. To my surprise, beneath all the swearing and spitting, there was a genuine revolt against the record and fashion industry. They were ripping off the young. Cynically manipulating the 'youth culture' to line the pockets of a few fat cats. Punk gave teenagers the chance to put two fingers up to the money men.

By the time I started to defend punk, Mark had opted out of it. The spell was broken for him at a gig in Alexandra Palace Park. First he found the event was sponsored by Marxists, whereas he was somewhere to the right of Genghis Khan. The death blow however came as he walked behind a young man. Admiring his metallic blue hair, it began to rain. Blue dye began to drip onto his shoulders proving he was a one day wonder. This small incident proved to Mark that the poseurs had arrived, designer punk was waiting in the wings.

Like his father, his commitment to the new movement was total. So was his rejection. To this day he is still known by some of his mates as 'Spike' because his hairstyle was a permanent feature. You see, after the boot polish job, Mark decided to go the whole hog and dyed his hair black, no rinses for him. Heaven only knows how they ever offered him a job.

The problem of being a leader is that, after a while, real feedback begins to dry up. Muswell Hill changed my isolation. Feedback was coming at me from all directions. My complacency was challenged. Forced to think again, my creative juices started to flow. One of the things I began to explore was the humanity of Christ. Centuries of Christianity had eroded it. To strip this man of his humanity is to deprive him of his greatness. To make him merely human is to rob him of his mystery.

Going back to the source documents, I began to read the accounts with new eyes. What emerged was a man of great independence and extraordinary courage. He was not afraid of creating a scandal or losing his reputation. No tradition was too sacred to be challenged. No concept too fundamental to be changed. No authority too great to be confronted. He was what all humans should be - an original.

Trying to restore the delicate balance between the human and the divine, I started to re-write the gospel. The result was called 'The Gospel according to St. George'. I have reproduced it as Appendix 2 to give an idea of my thinking at the time. Were I to tackle the task today, the result would be different as I have moved on. Nothing should remain static, not even a gospel. Change is essential to life. Stop changing and you start dying.

Some people were offended by my tongue-in-cheek title. Others felt it was a cheek to write my version of events when I was not there. As that did not stop Luke, I saw no reason for not trying. Paul's gospel was also a maverick. Bearing no resemblance to the other gospels is something he boasts about. Surprisingly there is not a quote from the lips of Jesus to be found in any of Paul's writing. Unwittingly I was reviving an old Gnostic tradition.

To promote my gospel, I decided to turn it into a multi-media presentation. Using the creative talents around me at Muswell Hill, we added dance and drama, music and songs. Initially it was a bit of a flop, but after we had honed it and added more humour it began to take off. On our final performance in Sheffield we had a standing ovation. People were amazed we were not continuing, but we felt we had exhausted all its potential.

Weddings are the events which flood into my mind when I think of the Muswell Hill fellowship. These were tailor-made to suit each couple. Ranging from ordered to chaotic, no two ceremonies were alike. Prophecy played a part in these weddings. But having learned to be naturally spiritual, none of the visitors noticed anything unusual. Eating together was at the heart of our communal activity and weddings reflected this. Instead of divorcing the ceremony from the reception, they were usually fused into one event.

Nothing was sacred to the Muswell Hill mob, anything could be challenged. Our large weekly gatherings were the first to come under the spotlight. Initially they had served a purpose, now they were beginning to be a chore. Worship was losing its creative edge and was becoming ritualised. So we scrapped these regular meetings, coming together only when there was some specific purpose.

Next we began to look at the sacred cow of the House Church movement - house groups. Splitting folk into groups had been done on geographical lines. Although it was the logical thing to do, it cut across the natural friendships that were being forged. Also the choice of leaders for these groups was a bit arbitrary. As they had not earned the respect their function called for, it all became rather artificial. Not only did we disband the groups, we asked all the leaders to stand down.

All this became too much for Dave and Hilary to cope with. Suddenly they confronted the church with the charge that I had led everyone astray during the last three years. This came as a shock not only to me, but to everyone as they had been part of the decision-making process. When they failed to get us to see the error of our ways, they left taking a handful of their closest friends. Although it was a small minority, the result was emotionally devastating. When the last of the bunch, Ian, said he was leaving, everyone burst into tears. Our bonding was deeper than we suspected. We were being torn apart - literally.

For me this was deeply traumatic. Dave had become my best friend, taking the place of Bob Finney. I had opened my heart to Dave and Hilary in a way I had never done to anyone else. All my doubts and fears were laid bare before them. Even my childish ambitions surfaced. Hilary once asked me what I would choose if money were no object. Without hesitation I said I would get a top of the range Porsche. I'll never forget the look of disappointment in her eyes, she expected something less materialistic from this 'man of God'.

To be rejected by people is never easy, but rejection from those you love is unbearable. I used anger to get me over the initial hurdle of grief, but it was only a temporary relief. About ten years later, Dave and Hilary invited me to lunch at my favourite Italian restaurant in Muswell Hill. It was an offer I could not refuse. Over lunch, they explained that they had now realised the error of their actions. They asked for my forgiveness in the most unconditional terms I have ever heard. We wept together.

But that was ten years away and didn't help at the time. Leaving folk to relate to whoever they wanted, deepened the bonds between us.

Friendship proved more cohesive than meetings. Meals took on a new significance. Communion wasn't a service you went to, it was a shared meal together. Laurie felt that wine was essential as it broke down the barriers between people. While a cup of tea has its place, nothing helps people lose their inhibitions like wine. *In vino veritas.*

Some people still felt the need to meet in groups and were free to do so. Others were relieved to be out of the pressure of a group. I admit to being in the latter category. Nobody raised the question, but my leadership would have to be reviewed soon. Having worked myself out of a job, I had become an optional extra in my own fellowship. Yet they still continued to support me financially, even though I was doing nothing locally. My time was now devoted to the other churches I was responsible for around the country.

FREEING CAPTIVES

'My father is a vicar and he thinks religion is a load of crap', said my daughter. Her RE teacher was stunned. Getting Sharon excused from religious education was a doddle after that. While she got my title wrong, she summed up my views on religion succinctly.

Carl Jung said religion is a defence against spiritual experience. I wholeheartedly agree. Most people are immunised against a real encounter with God by their priest dispensing his shot in the arm. Spiritual highs are available at a price. The price is determined by the job lot of beliefs you buy. The low church get their kicks from mass evangelism, the high church get theirs from the mumbo jumbo of the mass. In between these extremes lie a whole host of opiates for the people to try.

Dietrich Bonhoeffer, imprisoned for his part in trying to assassinate Hitler, had plenty of time to rethink his beliefs. He did. His exciting vision of a new Christianity is still a challenge fifty years later. Bonhoeffer's letters from prison not only display a warm humanity, but a spiritual daring we rarely see among pastors. His challenge to produce a religionless Christianity has never been taken seriously. The few who have done so use politics to fill the gap that religion left.

Our experiment in Muswell Hill is the nearest I had come to experiencing Christianity with all the props taken away. Baptisms were done in a bath, communion became a normal meal with wine, weddings were joy-filled events. We learned to celebrate life in all its rich diversity. Life is a great journey where you never arrive at your destination. To encounter God in the midst of everyday life is the ultimate experience.

While the Muswell Hill mob were blazing a trail, the other churches I was responsible for were struggling to keep up. The Woodford fellowship, for example, was grinding to a halt. As I could not put my finger on the problem, I asked Graham and Drew Phillimore to see if they could unravel the mystery. Graham had been at college with me, but it was not until he became the minister of a Baptist church a few miles from Chingford Congregational church that we really got to know each other.

Although he never joined the 'official' house church thing, his Baptist church was the freest I have ever seen. The relationships they encouraged among their members still flourish today. If anyone could get to the root of the Woodford malaise, Graham and Drew could. 'There is no fellowship there. They are just a group of individuals pulling in different directions. You are the unifying factor. Take you away and it falls apart', said Graham.

When I asked what he thought I should do, his answer was concise. 'Close it down'. Taken aback by his solution I did nothing. But after a while it became obvious it was a word of wisdom. When the moment came to announce its closure, I expected uproar. Instead my words were greeted with what amounted to a corporate sigh of relief. My learning curve was about to go up once again.

What amazed me was the mass return to the institutional church. The main beneficiary was All Saints, Woodford. Admittedly it was evangelical with a charismatic garnish, but it was Anglican. People obviously joined us for a variety of reasons. But I felt the common feeling was that the institutional churches were like prisons, most were delighted to be out. Here, at the first opportunity, all but a handful were heading back to jail.

Revelation came when I saw the film 'One Flew Over the Cuckoo's Nest'. To institutionalise a human being, either in a mental asylum or a religious order, you need to do three things: First, convince them that they are deficient mentally or spiritually. With the I-am-a-worm-not-a-man doctrine of evangelicals, this is a walk over. Next you prescribe a cure that is addictive and administered by others. Prayer, Bible study and regular services will do the trick. Finally, you con them into believing that passivity is the mark of maturity and you have them for life.

All institutions, not just religious and mental ones, thrive by giving us a deformed self-image. Even the great works of literature conspire to confirm that man's heart is deceitful and desperately wicked. Until you see the lie for yourself and discover the wonder that you are, you will keep running back to the security of the institution.

Dave Blackledge and his brother had been kicked out of their home by their parents. What crime can be so great that a mother can turn her back on the children she bore? Heresy. Yes, they had the audacity to disagree doctrinally with their parents. For most people that would put them off Christianity for ever. But David was willing to give it another try. He joined the Woodford fellowship and I spent a lot of time with him and his wife. Thinking I had imparted something of my anarchic spirit to him, I felt he would be able to survive outside mainstream Christianity.

Ten years later I received an invitation to his ordination into the priesthood. Where did I go wrong? He not only joined the local Anglican church, but had become part of its elite. At the service his wife asked me not to laugh when I saw him all robed up. She did when she first saw him in his new uniform. Wives help you to keep your feet on the ground. Actually he seemed quite soberly dressed when compared with those further up the hierarchy. Where did the bishop and clergy get those funny hats from? What do they feel all that dressing up like clowns does for them?

While I was able to wish David the best of luck with his new vocation, not all religious relapses were so benign. In another fellowship, Janette was also regressing. She was a wonderful wife and mother. Her house seemed to have the permanent smell of baked bread about it. The children were smartly turned out and well behaved. But one day, out of the blue, she said she was an evil mother and deserved to go to hell. The idea was so bizarre that I laughed when she first confided in me. But she was deadly serious.

Her background had been in a strange sect called the Exclusive Brethren. They lived by the letter of biblical law, never showing any mercy. These hard-line fundamentalists were hardest on themselves. When she and her husband joined one of our fellowships, they were like birds let out of a religious cage. Janette even danced before the Lord in her delight.

Suddenly she reverted back to the deformed self-image drummed into her when she was a child. Her self-worth was so low she felt she would be doing her family a favour if she killed herself. When she asked me what was the best way to commit suicide, I countered it by giving her reasons for living. But she had shut herself off. The local psychiatric hospital also did its best to help, yet she would not listen.

People often try to commit suicide to draw attention to themselves. Janette's first attempt appeared to confirm this. She jumped out of her first floor window. As it was only a few feet from the ground, she just ended up bruised. But one day her husband came home to find she had hanged herself from the banisters. I was gutted. At first I blamed myself for not taking her seriously enough. But those who did were no more successful. Later I realised that religion should carry a warning that it could seriously damage your health. My disenchantment with religion was now complete. I began looking for a way out.

Standing in the way of my exit were the fellowships I was responsible for. Muswell Hill was the exception. We were already experimenting with religionless Christianity and my leadership was surplus to requirements. What about the rest? Should I disband them as I had Woodford? While that may be the answer for a couple of them, it would be criminal to impose this on the rest.

All the churches I was responsible for were at different stages of development. The Sidcup fellowship had been forced out of their local church because of their involvement in the Charismatic movement. There was no turning back for them. Because of their history, they had been forged into a unity. Going their separate ways was unthinkable. I always enjoyed myself when I spent time with this group.

However, they were never able to leave their religious past completely. Free though they were in many ways, they never broke away from the system they were born into. Their meetings reflected this. Rather than force them to do things my way, I handed them over to John Noble's care. As his set-up had a more institutional flavour, they would be more at home under his 'covering'. It worked. So I began handing over other fellowships to leaders who were nearer to their way of thinking.

Although I had come to see religion as a dead end, I have never renounced living from one's spirit. On the contrary, spirituality is the only hope I have for man to get out of the chaos he is in. To me, spirituality and religion are not the same. Religion is like a mirror. Often its images of God and man are so distorted, it is only useful as a sideshow in a fairground. Even when the image is more accurate, it is still not the real thing. For that reason I have never been tempted to kiss my wife's reflection in a mirror. Were I foolish enough to do so, my lips would meet cold glass rather than the warm person I know.

94

All religions invite you to come through their looking glass into their own version of Wonderland. All sorts of goodies are promised if you are good. Sadly you only go through to the other side when you die. Who knows, you may have let yourself in for a never-ending Mad Hatter's tea party.

Spirituality, by contrast, is to do with living in the now. Its primary function is to enable you to experience eternity while you are still alive. Eternity is not a long time. It has nothing to do with time. Moving out of time, you end up in eternity. Dying is not the only way out of time.

Religion is like the moon, basking in reflected glory. It is a pale reflection which only shines in the dark ages of man. Spirituality is like the sun. The romantic in me cries out like Romeo:

> *'Arise, fair sun, and kill the envious moon,*
> *Who is already sick and pale with grief,*
> *That thou her maid are more fair than she:*
> *Be not her maid, since she is envious;*
> *Her vestal livery is but sick and green,*
> *And none but fools do wear it; cast it off'.*

MISSING, PRESUMED LOST

'Stop evangelising the world and start loving it.' That was the heart of my message on what turned out to be my last public appearance. As it was the start of the Decade of Evangelism for the 1980s, no one listened. Asking an evangelical to stop evangelising is like inviting him to stop breathing. So my colleagues have gone round in circles ever since - evangelical circles.

(My prediction that evening was that it would be a damp squib. Now the 1990s have been declared a Decade of Evangelism. Perhaps I was right. The irony is that I have just received a letter asking me to get involved indirectly. It was a request to use 'verses' from the Gospel according to St.George in an evangelical tract! I did not have the heart to refuse.)

Adding that we should 'love the world' made the alarm bells of Bible believers ring more loudly. St. John said we should not love the world, didn't he? But he used the word 'cosmos' which primarily refers to military or political order. My call was not to love the cosmos but the world of people. When you do you find they don't love the system either.

The political and economic systems that have evolved are based on certain values. As this impersonal machine has brought us to the brink of disaster, people are beginning to question its assumptions. Who is in control? To hide the fact that no one is, the powers-that-be blame 'market forces' for many disasters. The system is like some worldwide computer. Designed to service us, it has somehow taken control. 'You cannot fight the system', is the defeated cry. Christians should be pointing to the Christ who did. Instead they are demanding we submit to those in authority.

On that night ten years ago, all I was pleading for was a little understanding. My hope was to build a bridge between Us and Them: the church and the world. The bulk of my audience was drawn from the right wing of Christianity. Perhaps I sensed that this would be my last chance to speak from the platform I had helped build, so I covered a whole range of topics. Middle class morality masquerading as Christianity was one. The link between violence and the poverty trap was another. In all my years of preaching I had never been political. But talking about the problems of the world, you cannot avoid sounding political.

However the most damning part of my performance was when I held up a copy of *Playboy* magazine. Making it very clear that the nudes did not offend me, I pointed out what did. It was the whole ethos of the magazine. How dare they define what maleness was. Aiming to stop men maturing, *Playboy* was issuing a set of rules to keep men behaving like kids. For some that was no excuse for the public display of pornography.

At that meeting in the Westminster Central Hall I prophesied. Unless we get out of our cosy Christian ghetto, God will by-pass us. If we fail to get involved in the real world, He would use some other movement. God so loves the world that He will use anyone to help liberate it. Usually the most unlikely people. As my generation was too entrenched, I was aiming at the young. If anyone could break out, they could. 'Get out of the ghetto - God is giving us to the world', I cried. What was meant for others was about to boomerang back on me.

At the end the young applauded. The old guard sat on their hands. Maurice Smith was on the platform with me on that fateful night. Seven years later, after listening to the tape again, he wrote to me. 'I do not think many of us were ready to take in what you were saying then, in spite of the standing ovation', he wrote. 'Today I enjoyed every word and now understand the pathway you have trodden ever since'.
.
John Noble was probably the first to notice my change of direction. Partly because I was handing over some of my fellowships to his care, and partly because our apres-squash chats were becoming a bit stilted. We used to meet once a week for a game. What started out as a bit of fun had become a battle royal. It was as if we were trying to prove something to each other. Someone presented us with a belt and suggested we compete for it. Ultimately I won the belt, but it proved nothing. There was something brewing between us that could not be settled on a squash court.

Once again Fairmile Court was the venue. Concerned that I was moving away from him spiritually, John suggested I should move closer to him physically. He reasoned that, as I was no longer responsible for any fellowship, my talents could be put to good use at Romford. His concern for me was genuine, he was that kind of man. But my concern about what he was building at Romford surfaced.

What I saw when I first went there was unbridled freedom. Now that freedom had taken on a certain form. It had become institutionalised. John's stubborness meant the whole structure had an authoritarian flavour to it. Others had to give in to him, so he submitted to no one. To me, the most worrying part was their new project - a Christian school. While it might appear a noble aim to some, I saw it as evidence of a seige mentality. Separating the church from the world. Us and Them again. It was John's pride and joy - but I wanted no part of it.

All this burst into the open. A violent argument ensued. Probably because it was in public, we became polarised. Strong language was used. I confessed there was no way I would leave the Muswell Hill fellowship. It was my pride and joy. John was livid. In the heat of the moment he cursed me. 'I spit on your fellowship' he yelled. I stopped dead in my tracks. John's opinion was precious to me. Yet the man whose opinion I valued most was spitting on the best thing I had ever experienced. When we lose our tempers, we say outlandish things. But that strange sentence seemed to sum up John's attitude. Stunned into silence, I gave up the argument.

Decision time was dawning. The man who had faithfully stood by me from the beginning clearly didn't think much of my free-wheeling fellowship. The fellowship itself was supporting me financially even though there was nothing for me to do. My peers were sidelining me as I was 'too radical'! Evangelicals had long since written me off as a heretic. They were right.

Heretic is derived from a Greek word meaning 'able to choose'. Once I found I was free to choose, there was no holding me back. My next choice was directional rather than doctrinal. I chose to rejoin the human race and get a normal job. Probably that appears to be no big deal to you. After all it was merely a change of jobs. But after two decades of working within the Christian community, returning to the community of the world was a big step. Because we confuse identity with function, I felt something of my identity was lost in the transition. Back in the market place I felt like a stranger once again.

Getting a job was not easy either. For a short time I became an insurance agent but found this was not what I really wanted. Although there were loads of vacancies in the early 1980s, all the interesting ones were for the under forties. I was 45. With my tail between my legs, I asked my previous boss to take me back. Luckily he had forgotten my arrogant claim that God had called me to leave the murky world of commerce for higher things. But the old firm was a mere shadow of its former self.

Ardente Hearing Service was at its peak when I left, with over 100 consultants. Now there were only a dozen of us. Once I lost my self-consciousness and started to look around me, I realised there was no future for the company. It was dying on its feet. Three years later it filed for bankruptcy.

Now I was back in the swing of things, I decided to start up my own consultancy. The only question was where? For some time now I had wanted to leave London, it had lost its sparkle for me. But Dorothy loved it, particularly Muswell Hill. She was also back into the world of commerce again and had a very enjoyable job. We also loved our house. It was Edwardian and had character. Built on seven split-levels it made an ideal family home. With widely differing tastes in music, it meant we could escape from each other. The whole family loved the eight years we spent in it.

For my part I felt I was inhibiting the growth of the church being there. Some still deferred to me out of habit. Then there were the people from around the country still asking for my counsel. One couple came all the way from Edinburgh to submit to me. Imagine their shock when I told them it would be wrong for them to do so. Slowly I became aware that having to come up with answers was too much pressure. There were too many questions in my own mind. But the 'phone never stopped ringing. I felt peopled. I could not cope any more.

When I shared with Dorothy my need to get away, she felt that the time was right. What a relief that was. I ran out and put the house on the market. We anticipated that it would take at least a year to complete transactions at that time. Little did we know that everything would go through in a matter of weeks. We both agreed we should move nearer Dorothy's elderly parents, and selected the New Forest as the ideal venue.

On our very first visit to the New Forest we saw it: our dream cottage, complete with five-bar gate. Surrounded by an enormous hedge, it was wonderfully secluded. With its typical English country garden and fruit trees, we couldn't have asked for anything more. After almost a decade in the forest, we have not been tempted to move anywhere else. Within three months of placing our Edwardian residence on the market, we were living in our dream cottage. Perhaps God was also in a hurry to get us out of the way. But it was nevertheless a shock for the group in Muswell Hill that we left so swiftly.

Leaving the warmth of a caring community is disorientating. One minute you're in the middle of all the action, the next you are wandering aimlessly in the big wide world. As a fellowship we saw ourselves as fulfilling the purposes of God. On your own, life can appear quite meaningless. Having to earn some money brought some sense of normality into the situation. Going back to fitting hearing aids to the hearing-impaired was a relief. Here was something tangible where the results could be checked. Helping people to hear more clearly and getting paid for it was like having the best of both worlds.

The challenge of starting a business from scratch was also an exciting prospect. Exhibitions, arranged within a 30 mile radius of my home, proved to be a success. But using my home as a base was not. People telephoned all hours of the day and night. It was just like being a minister again. A few years later as my clientele grew, I changed all this and moved into consulting rooms in a lovely Georgian town ten miles away.

But events were very slow at the start. With plenty of time on my hands, things began to surface. Many of the hurts that had been hidden away in my subconscious came back to haunt me. Top of the list were the three rejections I had suffered at the hands of my friends. Bob Finney, Dave Mellows and now John Noble. Their reasons were all different. The impact was the same. Devastating. Emotionally I began to crack up. Like a wounded stag, I retreated deeper into the forest to lick my wounds.

Both my addresss and telephone number were a closely guarded secret. Close friends acted as filters to stop people getting in touch with me. How friends put up with my lack of communication I will never know. Writing letters was never my strong point, but now even the 'phone was an invasion of my privacy. We asked folk to leave us alone for one year.

100

Dorothy coped with the situation by going back to work. She had a very fulfilling job at Southampton University. She also joined the local drama group and played many roles, thoroughly enjoying herself. She became, in fact, the star of the family and I was known as 'Dorothy's husband'. Far from feeling upstaged, I began to enjoy my anonymity.

GLORIOUS ISOLATION

As my emotional barriers came down, my intellectual framework began to totter. What I really thought and felt came out into the open. Without the constraints of people hanging on to my every word, and the pressure of my peers, I was free to doubt. In the West we are forced to think in terms of opposites. Good and bad; light and dark; life and death; male and female; faith and doubt. Eastern thought sees opposites held together in dynamic tension. Faith and doubt are two sides of the same coin.

Doubt is a good way of uncovering truth. For me it was also cleansing. The final vestiges of guilt, built up by reading the Jewish part of the Bible, were washed away when I found out why it was included in the canon. Until the end of the second century, there was no attempt to have a written standard (or canon).

The first attempt was made by Marcion, one of Pual's disciples. It included most of Paul's epistles and the gospel written by Paul's friend Luke. At the time, Paul's writings were beginning to lose their general appeal. Marcion decided to stop the rot. Because he was a 'heretic' who had separated himself from Rome, taking a sizable chunk of the church with him, he was not allowed to get away with it.

The orthodox reacted. Strangely enough they used Marcion's list as a basis to build on. It took another 200 years for the list to be completed. First to be added to the heretic's canon were the 37 books of the Old Testament. That kept the Jewish lobby happy. Marcion had dropped the Jewish scriptures because he could not reconcile the God revealed in its pages with the Father Jesus proclaimed.

I must confess that I have always found the Old Testament hard to swallow, not just the bit about Jonah and the whale. Let me quote you a couple of verses from the second book of Kings as an example. 'Elisha left Jerico to go to Bethel, and on the way some boys came out of a town and made fun of him. "Get out of here, baldy!" they shouted. Elisha turned round, glared at them, and cursed them in the name of the Lord. Then two she-bears came out of the woods and tore forty-two of the boys to pieces'.

While I understand the prophet's lack of humour - most religious folk take themselves far too seriously - I was taken aback by the vicious response of Lord Yahweh. Forty two kids mauled for sending up a soothsayer? Obviously the Lord not only could not see the funny side of life, he also lacked compassion. How unlike Jesus.

Malcolm Muggeridge told me he had met many dictators and despots, and the one thing they all had in common was their lack of a sense of humour. Where does that leave Yahweh? Away from group pressure, I allowed myself the luxury of persuing this impertinent question. Squashing my instinct to make excuses for God opened the door to doubt. What kind of god is this? The question would not go away.

'He is a jealous God'. The verse from Joshua popped into my mind. Looking it up made things worse. '(He) will not forgive your sins. He will tolerate no rivals.' (24:19) Whereas I could see the need for anger, jealousy has always appeared such a childish, destructive emotion. Here it was compounded by a lack of forgiveness. Was this really the Father of the Son of Man? The final phrase, about not allowing rivals, smacked of insecurity.

Flooding into my mind came all the ethnic cleansing he initiated. Whole tribes wiped out at his command. The women and children were not spared. Yahweh's blood lust is seen most clearly in the sacrificial system he imposed on the Jews. His temple became a slaughter house. Innocent lambs were killed just to assauge his thirst for blood. Previously I had excused these gory practices on the grounds that they pointed to Christ, the Lamb of God. What seemed so profound, now looked rather shallow.

Facing the problem of suffering made me turn to the book of Job. This beautiful poem had often been a refuge when confronted with the suffering of innocents. Not this time. From my new perspective, God's treatment of Job was grotesque. Yahweh singles out his most devout servant and strips him of everything. After killing Job's children in quick succession, he forces Job to suffer a loathsome disease.

Although he uses a hitman to do his dirty work, it is ultimately God who gives Satan 'permission'. The whole thing was set up to win a bet with the devil. How capricious. Unaware that the roll of the dice has gone against him in the cosmic casino, Job takes an oath and swears his innocence. Jewish law forces the accuser to come up with proof of guilt or drop the charge. So the god of the Jews is forced by his own law to reply. To me he ducks the issue like an old pro.

Jews view suffering as a direct result of sin, either yours or your parents. Sometimes it can go back as far as four generations. But Yahweh can find no fault in his blameless servant. So after a guilty silence of almost thirty chapters, God points out that He exists. But Job never doubted that.

Next, God pulls rank and says he is in charge. 'How dare you challenge the way I run the world. You have no idea how difficult it is, my boy'. Behind all the beautiful poetry, that is the essence of Yahweh's reply. Once again you cannot help but notice the insecurity of the creator in all this. Job's question about the fairness of it all is never answered. He is forced to conclude that Yahweh is so powerful, no one can question his actions.

Finally, he bows to the might of the Almighty. What satisfied Job, left me cold. Nuclear weapons are all mighty, but only a nutter would worship them. The god of this tale is like some tin-pot dictator. Loyalty is more important to him than integrity. It is difficult to find any trace of the loving Father Jesus spoke of in this creator-god. He is more like a Mafia godfather than the Father I had come to know in my experience.

That experience also stood in the way of my becoming an athiest. Try as I may, I could not pretend God did not exist. Maybe he did not exist for others, but he did for me. On one of his rare TV apearances, Carl Jung was asked if he believed in God. 'I don't believe, I know', said the great psychologist with a twinkle in his eyes. Here was my problem. I did not have to prove to myself that there was a God, I knew he existed.

Mystics call what I was going through 'the dark night of the soul'. So I clung on to what one of them had said. 'The soul approaches God more nearly by not understanding than by understanding'. I was certainly not understanding. At this point I gave up trying. Why try, there were no answers. My depression deepened. So I decided to just live.

Hidden in my forest retreat, the television was my only window on the world. One Saturday I tuned into the biggest party ever held. Live Aid. It was a glorious summer's day in July 1985. Status Quo kicked off the proceedings. I felt my heart quicken as they belted out their familiar 'Rocking All Over the World'. Soon I found myself in tears. Nostalgia? No, the bands were not from my era. Emotional problems again? Not really, that was more or less behind me now.

Was it because the bad boys of rock were doing something positive? There was something of that in it, but there was a deeper root. It was Bob Geldorf's compassion. He vividly expressed it when he swore at the viewers. We had been slow to respond. Maybe it was just another publicity stunt. 'Get on the 'phones and give us some fucking money', demanded Bob. Niggling doubts fled before such genuine concern. Money began to pour in. Blind to what is acceptable, compassion uses any means to change what it finds unacceptable. Promises are never enough, it demands action.

Jesus healed people, not to prove who he was, but because he could not leave things as they were. 'He was moved with compassion.' It is difficult to express the Greek used here. Compassion is used to express those strong emotions that we feel in our bowels. Even 'gut reaction' is a bit weak. Compassion is an emotion which rises from deep within that cannot always be expressed prettily. Bob Geldorf is not a pretty sight. But the compassion I saw in the man made him beautiful. As I had never seen anything remotely attractive about the man, it came as rather a shock. What I had failed to find in the God of the Old Testament, I glimpsed in this self-confessed rat.

Gradually it dawned on me. When Jesus said 'the kingdom of God is within you', he was not having a private session with his disciples. He said it to the crowd. The kingdom he saw was in the people of the world, not locked away in the church.

How can you say God's kingdom is in the world when all we see is violence all around us? First, it is a bit over the top to claim violence is everywhere. The media love a good war. A war of words (they call it balance) is fine. But wars between families, between tribes, between nations are better, especially on TV. Bombs exploding and bullets flying are visually stunning. But the camera does lie. Journalists delight in being dramatic.

When the 'troubles' began in Northern Ireland, I began to wonder if I should stop preaching in the province. Basically I am a coward. Pretending to be brave, I carried on going to Belfast for many years. I am not saying that bullets do not fly, that bombs do not explode, that people do not get maimned or die. But fortunately, I never saw any violence on my visits, so it cannot be 'everywhere'. Asking why there is violence is as complex as asking why there is suffering. But I glimpsed a glimmer of an answer in an old Christian collection of the sayings of Jesus. 'If you bring forth what is within you, what is within you will save you', says the Thomas Gospel. 'If you do not bring forth what is within you, what you do not bring forth will destroy you'.

Within every man is the dynamic life of God. If it's allowed to flow out it gives life to everything you touch. Prevent that life from flowing out and it becomes life-threatening. Violence is the child of an unlived life. Seeing the kingdom of God everywhere and discovering the divine in every man was a new experience for me. I began searching for evidence of this kingdom in the oddest of places. I even peered into the enemy camp - science. I was pleasantly surprised by what I found.

PHYSICS AND MYSTICS

'God does not play dice', said Einstein. He refused to accept a universe governed by chance. Yet this was where his theory of relativity led. In his theory space and time are locked together, woven into the very fabric of the universe. Everything was relative. The speed of light was the only thing that remained constant.

Looking at light, scientists discovered it was made up of photons. These packets of light contain just the right amount of energy to carry out most chemical reactions. Light and life depend on each other. Einstein called these packets of energy 'quanta'. Quantum physics then stumbled on a paradox, the first of many. Sometimes light appeared to be a wave, at other times it appeared to be a particle.

Events like this led the scientist into the unfamiliar area of uncertainty. The clockwork world of Newton had to make room for the world of maybe. At subatomic levels, matter does not exist, it 'shows tendencies to exist'. Atomic events do not occur, they 'show tendencies to occur'. New physics had now embraced randomness and the roll of the dice. Underlying all of modern science is the uncertainty principle.

Newtonian physics still plays its part in our everyday lives. Mainly because our senses refuse to accept a world where solid objects are not solid and empty spaces not empty. But, during my lifetime, man's view of the universe has been turned on its head. Modern physicists' view of the world is strikingly similar to the way the mystics viewed it.

Now physics and metaphysics are converging. Take what one of the pioneeers of quantum physics said. 'What we observe is not nature itself, but nature exposed to our method of questioning. Therefore quantum physics leads to the only place to go - ourselves'. Now that I had the time, I set out on the search for the real me.

Self-discovery is always unsettling. You throw light on facets of your character that you wish had remained in the dark. Your shadow is never as attractive as the person you present to the world. We all want to be loved, so we screen off our unlovely bits. The socially unacceptable face of naked desire has to wear a mask to be invited to society's ball. But there is more to self-discovery than that.

When you explore the depths of your being, unknown dimensions also come to light. 'Let him who seeks continue seeking until he finds', says Jesus in the Thomas Gospel. 'When he finds, he will become troubled. When he becomes troubled, he will be astonished and rule over all things'. The astonishing thing is that while you search your human spirit, you stumble across the divine within.

Rediscovering the God within gave my spiritual life the kick-start it needed. Since entering the Christian fold I had been warned that I was just like a piece of coal. If I fell away from the fires of fellowship, I would grow cold and die. Maybe that did begin to happen. But now I was starting to self-ignite. Glowing inwardly is more healthy than having to cling to others for warmth. Feeling the warmth of my Father's smile was relief. No words were necessary. He knew. I began to enjoy a new lease of life.

In the summer of 1988, I was approached by a young TV producer. He was making a documentary on the movement I had left and wanted to highlight the submission issue. I jumped at the chance. Here was my opportunity to explain why I had quit. Nobody knew why I had vanished, now I could put the record straight. Or so I thought.

'We want to have you doing something natural as well as talking to camera' said the young producer. Rummaging through my leisure activities, we found we had something in common. Squash. 'You and I will have a game on camera', he declared. 'Natural' is not the word I would use for what followed. When we got on court, there were four other people there. The camera team had lined itself up along the front wall. Pointing out that their manhood could be at risk, we moved them over to one corner.

In the confined space left, it was difficult to do anything dramatic with the ball. 'Just pretend to hit it', they cried. Television is one great big illusion. After half an hour we managed to banish the camera team to the gallery. We succeeded in playing one game. Taking my frustration out on the producer, I thrashed him. He got his own back, the game ended up on the cutting floor. So did most of what I said.

For forty minutes I explained the movement and my part in it. Only four minutes survived. They were just dramatic sound bites. Far from

108

putting the record straight, it merely added to the mystery of my disappearance. As it was made for Channel 4, I found myself praying no one would watch it. At least no one who knew me. On Channel 4 that is not a tall order.

However, the young producer was trying to make a name for himself. So the film was transferred to ITV's documentary slot, 'First Tuesday'. To add to my chagrin the whole day's television on all channels was recorded for posterity. A kind of TV 'Domesday Book'. Perhaps if I wrote a book, I could have the last word. A major publishing house had already approached me. Knowing their evangelical bias, I knew they would reject my free-wheeling approach. But it was an idea. Perhaps one day.

At this stage even I began to wonder if I could still call myself a Christian. The only other person that I had heard of with a similar experience was George Fox. Like me, he believed in the Light within. But my beliefs were not static. They seemed to be continually evolving. As new evidence came to light, my conceptual framework was modified to accept it. Coming from a branch of Christianity which believed all the evidence was in, made me doubt my right to use the name 'Christian'. My doubts were about to be dispelled from a most unusual source.

Television is a boon to many of us who find it hard to switch off our minds after a hard day's work. Bland programmes fool the mind into thinking it is doing something. It is wonderfully soporific. Flicking through the channels in this mindless way, I chanced upon a glorious rarity - a thought provoking series. The subject was Gnosticism. What intrigued me initially was how they could make four hour-long programmes on a topic we dismissed on a single sheet of paper at theological college.

Within minutes I was hooked. There were Christians who felt like me in the early church! Later they were called heretics by the winners in the doctrinal stakes. But they never saw themselves as dissidents. Some even used the word 'heretics' when speaking of those we now regard as orthodox. Gnostics were primarily concerned with *gnosis kardia*; the knowledge of the heart. They claimed that to know oneself was not only to know human nature but, at the deepest level, to know God.

Beyond that simple statement, it is difficult to spell out what they believed. Their views, like mine, were continually changing. 'Every one of them, just as it suits his own temperament, modifies the traditions he has received. Just as the one who handed them down modified them when he shaped them according to his own will', complained Tertullian. You can see why this early church father was annoyed. How could you shoot at these Gnostics if they refused to stand still?

Another church father, Iraneaus, did try to blow them out of the water. His broadside ran to five volumes. Even its title was long. 'The Destruction and Overthrow of Falsely So-called Knowledge.' (The Greek word 'gnosis' means knowledge. Because it is not scientific knowledge, rather a knowing that comes from experience, it would be better translated as 'insight'.) But why should anyone, let alone a bishop, write five books to destroy a group of 'heretics'?

Gnostics were not some minor clique who could be easily written off. They were respected and influential. Valentinus, a Gnostic teacher and poet, almost became bishop of Rome. Imagine how the course of church history might have changed if this eloquent man had landed the top job..... But the Gnostics were not ousted because of their strange theology. They were caught in a political power struggle. Professor Pagels argues this brilliantly in her book 'The Gnostic Gospels'.

In the infant church, three broad streams developed. They first emerge in Paul's letter to the Corinthians. 'One says "I follow Paul"; another, "I follow Apollo"; another, "I follow Peter", another "I follow Christ".' Let us assume there is nothing wrong with following Christ and examine the other three.

Followers of Peter were part of a strong, militant Jewish contingent. Jerusalem was their headquarters. They appear to be as fanatical for the Law as the community at Qumran, where the Dead Sea scrolls were discovered. After the Romans razed Jerusalem to the ground, they held out for another seven years at Masada. Matthew wrote his gospel especially for this kind of group, peppering it with as many quotes from the Hebrew scriptures. They were the bane of Paul's life and vice versa.

Apollo's followers were the reverse Coming from a mainly Gentile background, they were suspicious of the Old Testament. Many wrote

110

their own gospels. If they had to plump for one written by the gang of four, it would be John's gospel. While the God of the Jews was wholly other, they emphasised the God within. Instead of sin and repentance, they talked in terms of illusion and enlightenment. With their total disregard for the Jewish law in favour of inner direction, they were set for a head on collision with Peter's friends.

Paul was not happy with either stream. He favoured a mix of Jew and Gentile. Finding a middle way between the two makes him the father of ecumenism. As a result, his letters are a confusing mixture of law and grace, of old style Judaism and exciting new 'insights'. For him God is both within and without. Probably his 'balance' helped Christianity survive but something was lost in the compromise - a spirit of adventure. Consensus replaced creativity.

The anarchic nature of Gnosticism contained the seeds of its own destruction. 'Whoever achieves gnosis is no longer a Christian but a Christ' said one of their number. You can almost hear the straight thinkers getting their knives out after hearing that. Their argument would be that it is better to lose these extremists than have the whole movement perish in the quicksand of mystical thought. By the end of the fourth century every trace of this 'heresy' had been wiped out by the 'orthodox'. Or had it?

Until recently, the best picture we had of the glorious diversity of early Christianity was painted by Iraneaus. It was extremely biased. Examining his jaundiced view of Gnosticism is like sifting through the writing of Ian Paisley to find out what the true Church of Rome is like. All that changed in December 1945. An Arab peasant stumbled across a treasure hidden in earthen vessels. The clay pots held manuscripts which were almost 1600 old.

The Nag Hammadi find shattered the illusion that there was a simple, uncomplicated form of Christianity in the early church. 'The fifty writings discovered at Nag Hammadi offer us only a glimpse of the complexities of the early Christian movement' says Christian historian Elaine Pagels. 'We now begin to see that what we call Christianity actually represents only a small selection of specific sources, chosen from among dozens of others'.

111

Not being an historian myself, the first sentence of the last chapter of her fascinating book was a revelation. 'It is the winners who write history - their way.' They present themselves as the heroes who banish the villains. Everyone likes to justify themselves. This book justifies the course of action I have taken. Many of my colleagues will say it is not a balanced view of the facts. 'There are no such things as facts', said the old journalist, Muggeridge. 'The whole thing is a great drama which we view from different standpoints'.

From my standpoint, Christianity was hijacked by the straight thinkers. What's more, they destroyed all the evidence. All Gnostic writings were burnt. But the inner light lived on it the heart of the mystics. Their God is not found in books, but in the fullness of their hearts. Others may believe, but the mystic knows. Because they soar beyond the confines of the mind, their experience is beyond language.

GNOSTIC ROOTS

Despite my flourishing consultancy business, my feet were kept firmly on the ground by the appalling state of the British economy. Just before things began to decline, I started a new business with my son. We chose the world of aquatics. My first mistake was I knew nothing about keeping fish: Mark was the expert. Ever since he was a little boy, fish had fascinated him.

He started by keeping sticklebacks in a tank in his room. He progressed to keeping a pike. Because pike need to be fed live fish, his friends loved calling round at feeding time. This was shortlived however. As soon as the pet-shop owner found out he was feeding live goldfish to the pike, he refused to sell him any more. Once he caught an eel in a local stream. Keeping it proved more difficult. Putting it in a special tank, he went to sleep. He was woken up by a strange noise under his bed. On investigation he found the eel was thrashing around on the floor. He put heavy bricks on top of the tank but the slippery eel lived up to its name. Mysteriously the creature still ended up on the floor. We were all pleased when he decided to release it back into the stream.

All this was fine, but does not help you to sell fish. My next mistake was to buy a franchise, thinking their expertise would help. To a limited degree it did. But becoming a franchisee is like signing up to join the army. You are given little choice. What is more, you have to work your butt off. I was not directly affected by the work-load. Mark was. We agreed that I would finance the deal, whereas my son would actually run the business.

Our final mistake was to believe the government knew what it was doing. Normally I dismiss what they say as lies. But as the Prime Minister was a whiz kid from the Treasury, I felt the economy was the one area he could be trusted in. Wrong again. He led us into the worst recession since the 1930s. Then he kept promising recovery was 'just around the corner'. It never came. What was alarming was the discovery that no one was able to take the helm as the economy headed for the rocks. Was there a helm or were we at the mercy of 'market forces?'

113

In the first year we lost money, but that was to be expected. We broke even the second year. Next year, we promised ourselves, we would make some real money. Instead, the business began to nose dive. Despite pouring money into it, it could not survive. We lost thousands of pounds. But Mark came off worst. Not only did he lose his job, but he lost his house. He was unable to pay the mortgage and like thousands of others, he handed the keys back to the building society.

It is difficult trying to make sense of senseless situations. Most of us have given up trying. Preoccupied with getting through the day and making ends meet, we lurch from one year to the next. Buried beneath the din of daily living is a still small voice, striving to be heard. 'Surely there is more to life than meets the eye?' But we choose not to listen. Accepting life is easier than questioning it.

Determined not to take the soft option, I set out to find some answers. I started with that old chestnut, why do the innocent suffer? C. S. Lewis' book *The Problem of Pain*, did not help. While it engaged my mind, it left my heart untouched. The play *Shadowlands*, which was the story of C. S. Lewis dealing with tragedy, shows that he failed to find comfort from his academic viewpoint when the chips were down. I have always found him sterile when he uses his logic, but stirring when he uses his imagination. *The Great Divorce* is an example of his fresh, striking imagery.

Turning to my new Gnostic source had the reverse effect. My mind was confused, but my heart was strangely warmed. They viewed creation as a cock-up of cosmic proportions. As a result, suffering is built into the very structure of the universe. Whoever is responsible for the lethal mix of fear, grief, pain and confusion in the world - it is not the Father whom Christ came to reveal.

Using myths, they explore that strange area outside the space-time dimension. Because it is so far removed from the world we know, there is no real way of describing it. So myths serve as an opening into that mysterious dimension which underlies everything. Unable to accept a god who created a world full of pain and injustice, they reject the creator while still worshipping the Father.

114

For us the words 'god' and 'creator' are so fused together that we cannot imagine one without the other. Splitting the atom is easier than divorcing God from the creator. The effect for me was just as explosive. The phrase 'let us make man' in the Genesis myth took on a new meaning. It pointed to more than one creator. Seeing creation as a result of flawed genius, opened up a whole new set of possibilities. Here was a group of early Christians throwing doubt on a fundamental concept of Christianity. I longed to share my findings with someone. But they were so bizarre, most of my friends would laugh at my naiveté. My grasp of these new ideas was so feeble, anyone could argue me out of them. Yet I knew I had seen something. What I needed was someone who would listen with their heart and not their head. Maurice Smith was that man. He was also one of the 'Fabulous Fourteen'.

Maurice had quit the new church movement soon after me. We felt it promised so much and delivered so little. Like me, he was emotionally shattered. Unlike me, he became concerned for the walking wounded of the house church. His gift is writing, especially letters. From his tiny almshouse near Canterbury, he began to communicate to the disenchanted. Obviously I was on his mailing list. Even though I rarely wrote back, he did not write me off.

Remembering his intuitive nature, I decided to contact him. Eileen, his long-suffering wife, said he was with friends on the Isle of Wight. As that was only half an hour's boat ride away, I arranged to meet him for lunch. We met in an eating house aptly named 'Gods Providence'. 'I've found my roots, Maurice', I blurted out; 'I've found my roots!' Then I proceeded to bend his ear for the next hour. He patiently listened to my faltering attempts to describe this anarchic form of Christianity I had unearthed. Because he trusts his heart more than his head, he also felt I was on to something.

It is not easy to explain why I was so delighted to find my experience mirrored in these heretics of the early church. Perhaps it was the evangelical in me - the inner promptings need external confirmation - having one last fling. Now I have laid that form of religious rationalism to rest. Doing away with external authority, you become a light to yourself. Living from the Source within, you become your own special creation.

Some of the Gnostic insights were obviously new to me. Separating God from the creator was one. Also the notion that we are outsiders in an alien world. Gnostics saw themselves as scuba divers, with their bodies acting as a life-support system. Providing it is properly maintained, you have the freedom to roam the seas. Exploring this strange underwater world can be a beautiful, moving experience. But they never confused the wetsuit with the person inside. So it is strange that gnosticism has become part of the job-lot we call New Age.

The term 'New Age' covers an enormous range of ideas. In my neck of the woods it is used of drop-outs driving broke-down buses. These New Age travellers are merely social security scroungers masquerading as anarchists. At the other extreme you have academics like Marylin Ferguson writing her impressive *Aquarian Conspiracy*. Not only is it intellectually honest, it is also stunningly provocative.

After reading through the wealth of literature flooding the market, a couple of themes begin to surface. First they claim 'All is One'. To them there is no difference between the person and the wetsuit. Old Age Gnostics would never accept that. Secondly, New Agers say that 'God is All'. He is an impersonal energy which permeates everything. It is a modern form of paganism worshipping nature with all her tyrannical power. To a Gnostic, the worship of raw power is revolting, whatever the source.

New Age gnosticism (with its celebration of the Eucharist), is stuck in a second century time warp. Once again it is stripped of its experimental nature. Here another truth about New Age becomes clear - it's not new. Old religions are wearing twentieth century clothes to sell their wares in the market place. New Age is not a religion as such. There is nothing called 'New Age' for you to join but you can belong to individual segments of it. The rituals of these sub-groups give the lie to its claim to be non-religious.

During my investigation of this new phenomenon, I decided that I needed some first-hand experience. The academic approach has never been my forté. As doctors were now encouraging their patients to try Transcendental Meditation, I thought I would try it too. I figured this had to be truly non-religious. First I had to part with a large amount of money. Nothing in New Age is free. I was then invited to a house in my locality. Ordered to bring fruit and flowers, I assumed they were for the owner of the house. But what was the white handkerchief for?

Fruit, flowers and white handkerchief were all used in a ceremony to obtain my 'mantra' from some 'ancient masters'. A mantra is a sound with no meaning. Although I took no active part, what I witnessed was an ancient ritual. As with all religious ceremonies, I found it difficult not to laugh. When the teacher left the room, I shared my misgivings with the group. A lorry driver, sent by his firm, agreed. 'I know why they get you to take your shoes off when you go in', he said. 'It's to stop you running away!'

Mantras are toys. They keep the hyperactive child we call 'the mind', occupied while we grab a few moments of peace. Toys are fine when you are growing up. New Age has all sorts of toys. Some, like playing with crystals, are harmless enough. But others like 'channelling' are not. Channelling is the new name given to the age-old practice of being a medium. My days as an exorcist alerted me to the dangers. Witches often attended my meetings in those days to argue with me. Strangely we agreed on one thing. Ouija boards were dangerous. What they called 'mischievous spirits' could damage the unwary. Why on earth they limited the danger to ouija boards heaven only knows.

Do not run away with the idea that I think the New Age movement is 'of the devil' as some claim. Far from it. I think it is the most exciting happening in decades. It has the same feel to it as the movement in the 1960s that gave birth to the Charismatic and Hippie movements. John Lennon summed up the spirit of that time in his evocative song 'Imagine'. Sadly the movement lost its momentum playing around with drugs. If New Age does not put away its toys it too will become obsolete.

Perhaps New Age is a signpost. Humanity is coming of age. Once we have passed through the teenage phase of trying everything to prove we are grown up, we will not need a signpost. The most exciting thing about this movement is the growing number of people who have an obvious spiritual dimension to their lives. Yet they have no contact with established religion. Here lies the hope for the future.

The Human Potential movement gave birth to New Age, because when you begin to explore your potential - you discover another dimension.

New Age delves into this hidden area. The most exciting challenge in this life is to explore this inner reality.

On the one hand, New Agers have a deep seated anxiety about this polluted planet of ours. Yet on the other hand there is the belief that we are entering a new phase in the evolution of the human race. We control it, rather than being controlled by it. To them the human potential is limitless. Rejecting external authority, they turn inward to seek guidance. 'Go where your intuition leads you', they say. 'Trust yourself.'

Somehow New Age thinking has permeated the highest bastions of America's business institutions. What the media calls 'New Age', is only the tip of the iceberg. The invisible nine-tenths is more important than the wacky visible tip. Why haven't we heard about this? Firstly, good news doesn't sell newspapers. Secondly, when the movement went within, the media couldn't cover it. Out of sight of most journalists, the iceberg is breaking away from its moorings. This mass movement - with over 100 million in its visible tip - is humanity declaring its right to explore spirituality in total freedom.

Science cannot tell us the meaning of life. It is not within its brief. This century began with the sweet taste of technology on our lips. As it ends, there is a bitter taste in our stomachs. Do not blame technology; it is neutral. The key is how we use it. The most exciting breakthrough of the 21st century will not be technological but spiritual. Our expanding sense of what it means to be truly human will break the mould.

As we approach the year 2000, many of us have a gut feeling that we are approaching a crucial turning point in time. Buffeted by change, our hunger for the spiritual intensifies. Faced with a world that appears to be spinning out of control, we realise the establishment has run out of ideas. In the next millennium, hierarchical structures will be forced to give way to more fluid networks. We desperately need to find the balance between being and doing.

CHRISTIANITY IN A NEW AGE

My experience of Christianity has been rich and varied. First there was my move from Anglican pew to nonconformist pulpit. Then out of the Charismatic movement, with its healings and exorcisms, into the house church movement where we tried to build caring communities; finally leaving the ordered world of fundamentalism for the anarchy of early Christianity. Being a pioneer in the House church movement helped me catch a glimpse of what the early 'church' was like.

Early Christianity had no shape to start with. Neither was there a generally accepted creed. There were no churches, just groups of people. Somehow their lives had been touched by Jesus, and they were looking for ways of expressing it. Others had been struck by what they had heard about this unique man. Although he had no coherent philosphy, Jesus' insights defy explanation. While acting with a total disregard for authority, this man spoke with great authority. Here was a man of great courage and independence. Unlike the bulk of modern church leaders - who are only just allowing women into their preisthood - he had no fear of the opposite sex.

Ordinary folk felt that if God was like Jesus (rather than the jealous One they had grown up with), then God was worth believing in. He translated what God felt into everyday language. The Word was being made flesh in him. Watching this process must have been fascinating. Jesus did not found a church - he started a movement. When that movement lost its impetus, it became part of the status quo it initially challenged. The church is merely a petrified form of an earlier vitality.

What most of us forget is that Christianity began as a Jewish heresy two thousand years ago. Perhaps a Christian heresy will be born which will serve humanity for the next two millennia. Christian revelation could add the warmth of personality to the cold 'energy' at the heart of the New Age movement. Hundreds of people who have survived death speak of seeing Light. But the Light is neither cold nor impersonal. They speak of encountering a Being of Light, even those who were athiests.

Unfortunately we cannot be sure that all the words credited to Jesus actually came from his mouth. Only the Spirit can bear witness to that. But a couple of phrases are used so frequently that they could be his. One is 'Son of man'. Unlike his followers, this was the way he preferred to describe himself. The other phrase is 'my Father in heaven'. Who better to reveal the Father than a Son? In John's gospel, Jesus said his Father was not to be confused to the exclusive father of Israel. The Jewish god was tribal, whereas his Father was universal.

The time has come to jettison the Jewish element of Christianity. Like a booster rocket, it helped to launch the new faith. When it had served its purpose, it should have been dumped with its load of guilt. Better late than never. Dropping Judaeo from Christianity will set it free to explore new frontiers. Morality was all right while we were growing up. Now we have come of age, we need to act like responsible grown-ups. By responsibility I am not advocating a new set of rules. I simply mean the ability to respond. New situations demand a flexibility that can flout the rules.

Jesus' words were meant to be life-giving. Some of his followers distorted them into a moral code. Because of the militant Jewish tendency of early Christianity, his words became set in stone. The spirit of what he said gives life, the letter kills. That is why he pointed to the kingdom within. Everyone has this inner capacity to find their own direction. 'Seek and you will find'. Within you is the light which enlightens everyone born into this world. Said Joseph Campbell:

'Anyone sensible enough to have looked around somewhere outside his fallen church will have seen standing everywhere on the cleared, and still clearing, world stage a company of mighty individuals; the great order of those who in the past found, and in the present are still finding, in themselves all the guidance needed'. (From the *Masks of God*).

The key is to start searching, not just for answers. Life is not a question to be answered, it is a mystery to be explored. Start exploring. Find new perspectives. Old assumptions are like familiar pieces of furniture. Most of the time we are unaware of them. These must be challenged. The easy chair of conformity must be taken out of our cosy cultural closet, and examined for what it is. Our conformity is due, in part, to our fear of ourselves. We doubt the rightness of our own decision and end up denying what we know in our bones.

All fear is fear of the unknown. Anything new is unknown. Out of our fear of the new, we perpetuate the known. The effect is deadening. Our entire culture is going through such traumas,it begs a new order. The known is failing, we must move into the unknown. We need to start asking questions in new ways. Look for new ways of seeing, new ways of knowing. Real learning - unlike gathering information - only occurs when we do away with authority. We must reclaim the power we have surrendered to authority. We are drowning in information, but starved of knowledge. Seek knowledge, especially of yourself. Discover that core of integrity within you that transcends all codes and conventions.

How can all this study-your-navel stuff help solve the world's problems? We are the world. What we see in the world is a reflection of ourselves. Stop wringing your hands and feeling impotent. Start with your own life. Remove the beam that obstructs your view of yourself and your purpose in life. With a clearer view, you can remove the speck from your brother's eye - if he asks you to.

With my track record, I would not blame you for thinking that I am after gathering another bunch of followers around me. Quite frankly, I have had enough of followers to last me a lifetime! What I am pleading for are seekers. Seekers are humble enough to admit they do not know everything. Whereas finders become keepers, keepers of what they believe to be the truth. Having found 'the answer', they stop looking. They set about trying to convince the rest of us they are right. Everyone must now subscribe to their belief system. Thus fundamentalists (religious or political) turn their friends into foes. Whereas faith is something you may be willing to die for, belief is something they are willing to kill for. All corporate violence is done in the name of some belief or another.

By remaining a seeker, you remain open to the fact that you might be wrong. You feel there is still something of substance you can learn from others. But to learn from one another, we need to stop being judgmental. No, I am not advocating we should become gullible, God forbid. What I am saying is we don't really listen to each other. We spend all our time accepting what fits in with our preconceptions, and rejecting the rest. To listen there must be an openess. Old ideas must be put aside to let the new flow in.

The brain has great difficulty accepting conflicting views. This is true of literal sight. When someone has double vision - if the brain cannot fuse them into a single vision - it will eventually repress the signals from one eye. Then the visual cells in the brain for that eye atrophy, causing blindness. In the same way the brain represses any information which does not fit into its conceptual framework. We all have a frame of reference. The trick is to make it as flexible as possible. So when the rational side of our brain conflicts with the intuitive, for example, we do not automatically side with the rational.

If the Charismatic movement (now well over 300 million) is to survive into the next century, it also must become flexible. Believing that its strength lies in its fundamentalist bias, charismatics cling to it. There is no denying that it has bolstered its incredible growth. But all kinds of fundamentalism thrive in time of great upheaval. Peddling their 'certainties', the traditionalists lay claim to the moral high ground. When things stabilize, as they will in time, fundamentalism loses its appeal. Once Charismatics discard their comfort blanket of 'certainties', they could start to build a Christianity without walls. If they are truly filled with the Spirit, change should pose no threat. With the Spirit of God, the unknown becomes friendly territory. Each fresh insight can then be examined on its own merits, rather than seeing if it fits in with some old concept. New ideas will enrich the movement, as well as enlarge it.

All this must sound heretical to any charismatic who has had the courage to read this far. Heresies always appear bizarre at first. Galileo found great difficulty explaining his new perspective. Mankind had always believed the sun orbited the earth. Anyone with eyes to see knew man was right. Yet they were mistaken. What sounded crazy when first aired, we now take for granted. The Roman Catholic church has taken over three centuries to forgive Galileo for being right.

Mankind also took a great leap forward when we learned to light our own fires. Instead of waiting for lightning to strike, man struck two pieces of flint together. From that moment on we began to move towards controlling our own destiny. Modern man is now learning to light his own spiritual fire, without the help of religion. Ultimately that will transform the way we perceive things. We desperately need this spiritual renaissance to meet the challenges of the new era. Life is growing more complex by the minute. The simplistic morality of our ancestors cannot cope with it. With our growing ability to manipulate life - and one day create it? - we need an evolving spirituality.

Spiritual life is a fire. It has an energy, a burning quality. Religion is merely the ash left by encounters in this realm. The time has come to stop poking around in the ashes of other people's experiences. Do not accept someone else's agenda, find your own. Discover the fire within. No matter who you are, you will find you are God in your deepest identity.

> *'I have faith in all those things that are yet to be said.*
> *I want to set free my most holy feelings.*
> *What no one has dared to want*
> *Will be impossible for me to refuse.'*

Rainer Maria Rilke

POST SCRIPT

While writing the final chapters of this book, I attended some lectures on Jungian psychology. The lecturer, a Roman Catholic priest, was excellent at interpreting psychobabble to the ignorant. Archetypes, the Collective Unconscious and many other terms were put within reach of the conscious mind. Often he would use Jung's own life as an illustration of what he was saying. (Jung's psychology is based on his own personal experience.) At other times the lecturer would use his intimate knowledge of African tribes to illumine the depths of the psyche. One day he used an illustration that was so different, it was almost jarring.

'Two caterpillars went for a walk', he said. 'As they were strolling along, they saw hundreds of other caterpillars all heading in one direction. "Where are you going?" said the first caterpillar. "To the top of the mountain," said one of the horde. "Why not join us?" After a bit of consultation, the two friends decided to throw in their lot with this mass movement. Mountains have a magnetism that is hard to resist. At first, they were carried along by the enthusiasm of those around them. Others may wander aimlessly, but they were going somewhere.

'Then the second caterpillar felt a bit uneasy about the direction they were going in. "Of course it's all right," said his friend, "There's the mountain." Standing at the foot of the mountain, number two still had his doubts. "Why are we climbing this?" "Because it's there," they cried in unison. Standard answers no longer satisfied him. "I'm heading off to the forest," he said, "are you coming?" But the first caterpillar felt it would be letting the side down to leave now. So he stayed on, while his friend headed off to the lush forest.

'After a great deal of hard slog, they reached the summit. Although the view was beautiful, the mountain top experience wasn't all it was cracked up to be. Many had died on the way up. Number one began thinking about his friend. "I wonder what he's doing now?" he thought. "Probably nothing - just laying on a branch, nibbling the odd leaf or two." In the midst of all the hectivity, he knew he was in the wrong place. Setting out to find his friend, he felt a great sense of relief. On the way down, the

124

walking wounded he met only served to confirm his decision to quit.

'After making a few enquiries, he found number two hanging from a branch, slowly wrapping himself in a fine covering. "What are you doing?" "Well, I've been sitting around here for long enough," said his friend. "I fancy a bit of a change." "I think I'll join you," said number one. "I wouldn't mind hanging around here for a while myself." Slowly he began to spin a silky cocoon around him to protect his fragile self. The transformation was absurdly simple. One day, he thought, I'll fly away.'

Though I cannot remember the point of this quaint little story, I felt my life had just flashed before me.

125

APPENDICES

APPENDIX 1

ANOTHER DAY
Song written by Dave Bryant December 1990

We were young, the night was old
We saw a brand new day unfold

As we stood in the rays of a rising sun
Our hearts were warmed and our minds were one

We were born to a crazy dream
To build a kingdom that would reign supreme

We rode out on the crest of a wave
We had a mission and a world to save

WHERE HAS IT GONE
IT'S BEEN SO LONG
SINCE WE'VE BEEN MOVING ON
TO ANOTHER DAY

We drew up along the battle line
Banners waving as we marched in time

We were the ones to make all things new
We were led by the chosen few

Driven onward by wind and fire
Our eyes were blazing and our guns were for hire

So much to strive for, so little to show
Eager children impatient to grow

NOW IT'S ALL GONE
LIKE A FADED SONG
AND WE'VE BEEN MOVING ON
TO ANOTHER DAY

We'd sing and dance into the night
We were living at those dizzy heights

Reaching out for the stars and moon
We were certain He was coming soon

Trying to hold to the trail we blazed
Easy joy became a masquerade

We moved too fast and we tried too hard
The kingdom dream became a house of cards

NOW IT'S ALL GONE
LIKE A FADED SONG
AND WE'VE BEEN MOVING ON
TO ANOTHER DAY
AND AS THE SYMPHONY
CONTINUES CHANGING KEY
WE'RE MOVING ON TO SEE
ANOTHER DAY

APPENDIX II

The Gospel According to St. George

Another Gospel?

Not really. Each gospel is not merely a collection of data, but an expression of the writer's relationship with Christ within the framework of his own culture. That is why John's gospel is so different from the rest. He wrote it much later than the others and to another culture. They all felt free to adapt the story to their time.

Two thousand years of history have passed since the great event. We no longer live in a world where spiritual reality is part of the fabric of life. Materialism reigns. Man has grown up without getting better. Disillusionment has set in. In the following pages, without changing facts, allowances have been made for the changes that have taken place on earth.

Buried under a mound of religious rubbish is something really precious. Few have the time to search in our fast moving society. So I decided to strip off the wrapping paper. Having done that, I am at a loss fully to describe what I see. For there is an element of mystery about this man that is truly fascinating. He spoke in parables which floored both wise and simple alike, and he rarely justified what he said. My hope is that something of the fresh originality and creative diversity of this timeless man is captured on the following pages.

BC-AD

One man in history has changed the lives of more people than any other. Towering over the giants of history, He is a challenge to those who are making history today, for no one interested in life and its ultimate questions can ignore him. Although he never wrote a book, more books have been written about him than anyone else. There has never been a man quite like Jesus of Nazareth.

When most people think of him it is always in a religious context. Yet he really threw his opponents by his non-religious way of life. 'Our disciples pray and fast', they said. 'Why are yours wining and dining?'

iii

His reply was fascinating. 'You cannot put new wine into old wine-skins.' Put another way, he was telling them they could not contain what he was doing in a religious framework.

New Kind of Freedom

He brings a quality of freedom that radically alters all other concepts of freedom. Not being bound by the law of logical alternatives, he seems not to be a man of principle. Keeping company with the wrong kind of people and refusing to do the right thing he ended up with the title 'prince of evil'! When the reality of that begins to hit you, you realise what a threat he was to the system.

Some of the most frightening things he said were not aimed at the sinners, but at the religious leaders of his day. It is easy to see why the establishment wanted to get rid of him at all costs. This unpredictable man was an enigma to them. He just did not fit their notion of messiah, so they killed the Messiah in order to keep their concept.

Invading Planet Earth

The awesome truth is that the person who created the universe, locked himself into our time-space world. He ate and drank, worked and played on this planet just like you and me. The infinite became finite.

Yet he started with no divine rights. In fact he got off to a bad start. Born in a smelly stable in the small town of Bethlehem, he was part of the most hated race the world has ever known. Throughout life he bore the stigma of being conceived outside marriage, for who ever heard of a virgin giving birth. However, from the darkness of Mary's womb, this Being of light was to illumine our darkness.

(By the way, he was not born on 25th December. That was the day when the pagan world celebrated the birth of their sun-god. Not wishing to upset the status-quo too much, the institutional church claimed that Jesus was born on the same day. In doing so, they neatly side-stepped the fact that it would be too cold for shepherds to be in the fields with their flocks — even in Israel.)

iv

'The Word Became Flesh'

There was nothing physical to mark this man out from other men, although the Samaritan woman knew he was a Jew without being told. His clothes were in keeping with the time in which he lived, though the cloth was of such quality, that when he died, the soldiers refused to rip it up.

In the art galleries of the world you will see pictures trying to capture the presence of this unique man. But bright halos fail to catch the mystery of the eyewitness account. 'So the Word became flesh and pitched his tent among us, and we saw his glory'. This glory that John saw was not some eerie aura, but the interaction of the human and the divine. He saw in Jesus the nature of God focused into one human being, and it was simply glorious. It resulted in a totally new kind of man...

The Hidden Years

The only glimpse we are given of his childhood is when his parents lost him after his Bar-mitzvah! When they eventually found him, after three days of anguished searching, it was in the place where many of us would have looked first of all, the temple. Yet to those who knew him well, it was the last place in the world they expected to find him. That is the first hint we have of the non-religious nature of Jesus.

Finding job satisfaction as a carpenter, he seemed content to spend the next eighteen years exploring his new relationship as a man with his heavenly Father. We are told that he learnt obedience through the things that he suffered. Part of that suffering must have been his burning desire to make men whole being held in check by the fact that his time had not yet come. Day by day the lame, the blind, and the bruised went by the door. Yet he did not heal one of them.

Naturally Spiritual

When his time arrived, it was marked by the friendly voice of his Father saying from Heaven, "This is my beloved son and I am wonderfully pleased with him!" He said that before his son had done anything. Father was commending him for the job he did best — living. He really enjoyed it. Having majored on his being a man of sorrows (one of the

v

many facets of Jesus), we have ended up with a caricature of the man. Kids do not respond to gloomy people, but they were naturally drawn to him. The truly spiritual man can be sad and full of joy at the same time.

'In him was life' said the man who knew him better than most. Jesus was a therapeutic person, it was just good being with him. He did not have to say a word. While others were content to exist, this man lived life to the full. To him eternal life was not just a quantity of time later but a quality of life now. Many stop living just to be 'spiritual' whereas this man lived in a way that was naturally spiritual. He was a master in the art of living. His purpose in coming was that we should have his overflowing life.

Marked Contrast

The picture most have of Jesus is that he was a modified, more gracious version of John the Baptist. Yet the contrast between the two is remarkable. John began his ministry in the lonely deserts of Judea: Jesus started more gregariously. He went to a wedding feast in Cana. When the wine ran out, the pious people must have breathed a sigh of relief. Not the Master — he made a further 180 gallons of vintage wine. Teetotallers have been trying to change it back to water ever since. Failing that, they like to pretend it was really grape juice.

In marked contrast to the austere life of John. The Son of Man came eating and drinking. So they called him a glutton and a drunkard. The devout recognised the disciples of the Baptist for they prayed and fasted. What they could not understand was what Christ's disciples were doing always wining and dining. When challenged about their lack of ritual, the Master said he had not come to patch their old systems, but to introduce a brand new way of living. Religious men live by concept. So when they could not fit the new ideas into the old they abandoned them.

His Radical Approach...

Jesus rejected the idea of a religious code that was both abstract and uniform. The law was not a dead letter but a living thing. So he felt free to change it. 'The laws of Moses said ... But I say ...' He speaks with a freedom that is not bound by the law of logical alternatives. In this freedom Jesus leaves all laws beneath him. To the Pharisees this appeared to be the reverse of all that was decent and orderly. Because he refused to play the game by their rule book and conform with their concept of goodness, they said, 'This man is not from God, for he does not keep the Sabbath'.

Not only did he seem to condone law breaking, but the Master defied the law of necessity all along the line. If the sin of hand or eye was impeding your freedom, he taught that you were better off without it. When money became a necessity, he said you should give it away. He not only lived free of all the ordinary pressures of life, but encouraged others to do the same.

'Do not ask anxiously, "What shall we eat? What are we to drink? What shall we wear?" All these things are for the heathen to run after, not for you, because your heavenly Father knows that you need them all. Set your mind on God's kingdom and his justice before everything else and the rest will come to you as well. So do not be anxious about tomorrow: tomorrow will look after itself. Each day has troubles enough of its own.'

... Had a Revolutionary Impact

Following this man has meant a radical change in lifestyles not only of individuals, but also of communities. However his ways of revolution are more subtle than those of other men. In the end they are far more effective, for he is not satisfied with changing men's minds. His target is their hearts.

Consider the way in which he began the emancipation of the women in a culture which believed they were 'made simply to bear children'. He took them along as part of his team. Sometimes they appeared to understand the Son of Man more clearly than the men. Mary, for instance, knew he would die: a fact the men refused to face up to. So she did to his living body what people do to the dead. She anointed it with spices. As things turned out, they never had a chance to embalm his corpse — he did not stay dead long enough.

It is also recorded that Mary 'sat at the feet' of Jesus (as Paul did with his teacher Gamaliel). Her sister Martha was shocked that she had quit her womanly role, and played the man's part. After appealing to this Rabbi she was even more shocked. Having told her to stop fussing like a mother hen, he added, 'The part Mary has chosen is best, and it shall not be taken away from her'. Until that moment this 'part' had been the exclusive domain of Jewish males. The movement to liberate women from being the slaves of men had begun.

Far-Reaching Implications

The prophecy given at his birth was that he would bring down 'the monarchs from their thrones.' Who could have guessed that he would do that while answering a question on taxation? 'Pay Caesar what is due to Caesar and pay God what is due to God'. What seemed like the Master getting himself out of a tight spot, turned out to have far-reaching implications. Separating the church from the state, he was paving the way for a society in which no man ever ruled by divine right.

The early Christians began to put this into practice when they agreed to pray for the emperor, but they flatly refused to burn incense at his altar. By doing this they gave him authority, but at the same time they set out a boundary. Their loyalty to a heavenly King could only grant conditional loyalty to any earthly ruler. This subverts the nationalism that is required to build a strong state. Any totalitarian regime must always deal ruthlessly with the followers of this man.

Unconventional

Although we are born originals, most of us end up as copies. This could never be said of Jesus. Just the way he lived threw up problems. His friendship had no ulterior motive. He just wanted to be friends, even with sinners. This was a constant source of embarrassment to his disciples, until they grasped something of the all-embracing heart of this man. His love knew no boundaries. It extended not only to those who loved him, but also to those who would betray and crucify him. To him everyone was 'in' until they declared themselves 'out'. The Master managed to accept folk as they were, while not losing sight of what they would be. 'You are Simon (a reed), you will be Peter (a rock)'.

In his pursuit of people etiquette often went by the board. Once he allowed a prostitute to wash his feet with her tears, wipe them with her hair, kiss them with her lips and finally pour her perfume all over them. When his host got up tight about this, he did not placate him. If anything, he made it worse by pointing out the deficiencies of his host. The last straw was when he turned to the woman and did that which only God can do — he forgave her sins. He seemed set on a collision course with institutionalism, refusing to be bound by their legalism.

Inconsistent

'Master, this woman was caught in the very act of adultery.' One cannot help but wonder what happened to the man.

'In the law that Moses has laid down, such women are to be stoned. What do you say?' How does he respond in this pressured situation? By doodling in the sand! When they urge him further he says he will allow anyone there who is faultless to throw the first stone. The older ones slip away because they know when they are beaten. The younger element, being more arrogant, linger on until something of the perfect integrity of the man compels them to leave also. At this point Jesus should have stoned her. Not only because the law demanded it, but also for consistency's sake — he was the faultless one. However, faced with the alternatives of upholding the moral law or abandoning it to the ethics of the situation he holds the two in tension.

'Has no one condemned you?' 'No one, sir', she answered. 'Nor do I condemn you. You may go, but do not sin again.'

His Kingdom

'The time has come, the kingdom of God is here'. That is how the Son of Man ushered in the new age. The God he spoke of was not some tribal or national god, but the God of the universe. Right from the start he was calling the whole human race to himself. 'From east and west people will come', he prophesied, 'From north and south for the feast in the kingdom of God.' There were to be no barriers of race, class or sex. The old Jewish society was controlled by static laws which were imposed from outside. In the new society men would respond from a dynamic urge within. Instead of presenting a new set of writings, he offered a new relationship with the Writer. The message would not be carved from stone. It would be written on the hearts of men and women. He promised a new heart which had everything built in.

There was no cheap way into his society. It was easier for a camel to go through the eye of a needle (an Arab joke) than for a rich man to enter. Why? Because he would have to sell all and give it to the poor. The basis of our society is money whereas love is the foundation of his. For love placed you in a right relationship with God and man.

Difficult To Get In

The Master never pretended that following him would be easy. 'Come with me and I will make you fishers of men.' That was not said to just anyone, but to seasoned fishermen. They knew he was calling them to a life commitment not a leisure sport. There is a world of difference between a picnic on a sunny river bank when you feel like it and risking death on the high seas. He was in the risk business and it would not be a picnic.

'I'll follow you, sir', said the keen volunteer. 'First let me say good-bye to my folks at home'. But Jesus said, 'No one who sets his hand to the plough and looks back is fit for the kingdom of God.' Jesus took the initiative with another and said, 'Follow me'. 'Let me go and bury my father first.' Again it was quite a normal demand and yet the reply was strange. 'Leave the dead to bury their dead; you must go and announce the kingdom.' Was there a lack of compassion in the Son of Man? Of course not. What we see here is the degree of commitment he wanted, fused with the urgency of his task.

Easy To Get Out

Even when that commitment was made, he still made it easy to opt out. Unlike the cults, which make it easy to get in but treat a defector as an enemy to be punished. Once, after he had fed thousands of people, they got carried away and wanted to make him king. His response was incredible. 'Unless you eat the flesh of the Son of Man and drink his blood, you shall not have life within you.' No explanation was offered. They were left with this bald invitation to eat him. Although we can understand being revolted by the thought of eating human flesh, no Gentile can fully grasp how revolting drinking blood is to a Jew. 'This is more than we can stomach!', they cried as they withdrew from the man they were about to crown as their king. Still not explaining what he meant, he turned to the Twelve. 'Do you also want to leave me?' he asks.

Simon Peter's answer is superb. 'Lord, to whom shall we go? Your words are the words of eternal life!'

The Alternative Society

Standing before the representative of one of the greatest empires the world has ever known, Jesus declared that his kingdom is not of this world. 'If my kingdom were from this world my servants would be fighting to free me. My kingdom is not of this realm.' The proof of this other dimension was clear when he preached the good news of the kingdom. On these occasions people were always healed and evil spirits thrown out. 'If I cast out demons by the spirit of God, then the kingdom of God has come upon you.' he said. This supernatural activity was the display of the unseen realm crashing in upon the seen.

There was this sense in which the kingdom was here and now; in proclaiming it he was also looking forward to the time when the warring nations of this planet would stop destroying each other. So he taught his disciples to pray 'Thy kingdom come'. For he knew only the peace and justice of God's kingdom could stabilise the earth.

Unorthodox Teacher

He spoke in parables that the crowd should not understand. The reason for this is that he is after men's hearts not just their heads. The parables seem simple enough, yet they were so profound that even his disciples had to ask him to explain them. As their hearts were open, he was prepared to go into detailed explanations for them.

Rarely did he speak at a meeting geared for preaching. A lot of his words were provoked either by a question, or the situation in which he found himself. At times the crowd were spontaneously drawn to him. The people were astonished by his teaching. Unlike their own teachers, he taught with a note of authority. His use of the word 'Amen' is interesting. The Jews used it to affirm or endorse the words of another. This teacher used it exclusively to introduce his own words, showing his authority was not derived from anyone.

Their teachers would also give straight-forward answers to their enquiries. The Master often threw the questions back to them at a deeper level.

When a lawyer asked 'What must I do?' The Master replied 'What does the law say?' 'Love God and your neighbour' replied the lawyer, 'But who is my neighbour?' After telling the story of the Good Samaritan, he tossed the question back. 'Which of these men was neighbour to this man?' He was forcing the man to commit himself by choosing.

Unpredictable Mover

When healing people the Son of Man was very unpredictable. Sometimes he would heal just one: at other times he would heal the lot. He lacked any modus operandi. Take his method for healing the blind. He cast a demon out of one, but to another he spoke a word of faith. There were occasions when he simply touched their eyes. Once he went as far as spitting in a blind man's eye. Finally, there was the incident when he spat on the ground, made a paste with the spittle and then spread it on the person's eyes. I have seen many Christian healers in action but I have never seen one do that!

'They are all looking for you', said Simon. 'Then let us move on', replied Jesus. The nearest he came to explaining his movements was when he said: 'The wind blows where it wills; you hear the sound of it, but you do not know where it comes from or where it is going. So it is with everyone who is born of the Spirit.'

Living For Others

To see him move was to see love in action. The patience of Jesus with ordinary people seemed inexhaustible. Wherever he went he put a value on people's lives. He was delighted when folk got it right and were full of faith. His compassionate heart was always looking for ways of being positive. Often he would anticipate needs in advance. Like the time when the thousands following him forgot to bring their food. Not only did he provide enough to satisfy everyone, but there were twelve baskets left over. That is not bad when all you have are five loaves and two fishes to start with! He also obviously did it without a lot of fuss, for his disciples still panicked when confronted with a similar dilemma. 'How can we provide for all these people?' they cried. This time there were seven baskets more than they needed. He just could not think economically.

There is something delightfully extravagant about all he did for others. Nowhere is this more evident than when he healed the sick. It is staggering to think of the vast numbers he made whole. No one who came to him for healing was ever turned away. There is no record of anyone losing their healing, not even the nine lepers who forgot to thank him.

This servant attitude of Jesus was the mark of his true greatness. He was a man for others. He was not role-playing when washing the disciples feet. He was being what he was — the supreme servant. 'The Son of Man did not come to be served but to serve.'

Very Provocative

A man with a withered hand stood before him on the Sabbath. The Pharisees were more concerned with the principle of law than with the plight of this man. The record says that this man from Galilee looked 'round at them with anger and sorrow because of their obstinate stupidity'. Now he could have left it there. He did not. He deliberately healed the man knowing it would provoke them. He knew they would not see a healed body, all they would see was a broken Sabbath. So the scripture-loving Pharisees joined forces with the politically-motivated Herodians (whom they despised) in order to destroy this man. For he was (and remains) sudden death to every rigid structure which seeks to preserve itself rather than the people it is supposed to be caring for.

Terrifyingly Tough

While he was a gentle man in many ways, in other ways he was terrifyingly tough. On two occasions he cleared the temple area of traders; once at the beginning of his public life, the other at the end. Although he saw the exploiting of man as a crime against God, what he could not stand were those who were serving God for personal gain.

However, it was not only his actions. Some of the most frightening things ever said came from the Lord's mouth. He spoke of the realities of hell more than anyone else in the Bible. The alarming thing is that these words were not spoken to the sinners, on the contrary, they were addressed to the church leaders of his day. The language he used to denounce them was often very scathing.

'You Pharisees! You clean the outside of the cup and plate; but inside you there is nothing but greed and wickedness. You fools! Did not he who made the outside make the inside too? Alas for you Pharisees! You pay tithes of mint and rue and every garden-herb, but you have no care for justice and the love of God. It is this you should have practised, without neglecting the others. Alas for you Pharisees! You love the seats of honour at the synagogue and the salutations in the market-places. Alas, alas, you are like unmarked graves over which men may walk without knowing it.'

It is easy to see why the religious hierarchy of his day wanted to get rid of him at all costs. He was a complete enigma to them.

Life After Death

No man ever spoke like this man for his words were life to his hearers. Never was this more evident than when Jesus met a dead body. He seemed unable to accept the inevitability of death as others did. No funeral arrangements were safe with him around. On arrival at the house of the president of the synagogue, he was greeted by the noise of the mourners wailing. Laughter breaks out when he says she's not dead but sleeping. So he sends them packing and starts speaking to the corpse. 'Get up, my child.' And much to everyone's surprise - she does.

The ceremony had gone a bit further with the widow of Nain's son, the cortege had reached the city gates before Jesus interrupted it. Putting his hands on the coffin, he addressed the occupant. 'Young man rise up!' When the young man did a deep sense of awe fell on all who had gathered to pay their last respects to the dead.

'Dig Him Up!'

Lazarus is the most famous example of this prince of life interfering with death. As the Master had deliberately delayed his coming, they had managed to put him in the grave this time. 'Take away the stone' should really read 'Dig him up'! Nothing was sacred to this man. Martha, practical as ever, protests that the stench of a four-day old corpse would be unbearable. But he was not expecting to see a dead body. 'Lazarus, come out,' he shouted after they had removed the stone. It was good that the Master named his friend for he could have got more than he wanted...

The sight of a man coming out of a dark tomb, covered in bandages from head to toe, must have been frightening. However they soon got over the shock and celebrated this great victory over death. All except the religious leaders. They resolved to put to death the newly-raised Lazarus as many Jews were putting their faith in Jesus because of this man. When the system cannot control something it must suppress it. If life is causing the problems, then they must kill it.

Facing Death

The first (and possibly only) sermon Jesus preached in his home town produced a dramatic reaction. The people were so incensed with what he said that they wanted to kill him. The town was built on the brow of a hill, so they decided to throw the local boy off the cliff. Then, for some inexplicable reason, they let him walk away free.

One time in Jerusalem he declared 'My Father and I are one!' There was no mistaking what he meant. The crowd picked up stones to hurl at him. The penalty for blasphemy was death, yet once again it came to nothing.

The Master walked away from death on many occasions. He was not afraid to die, but his Father had given him the right to determine when it should happen. When the moment came it did not shatter him. Out there in the desert, before he began his public ministry, he was tempted to take the short cut and avoid the sacrifice. So he faced up to death right from the start.

Later, when he was trying to explain to his disciples that he was to be sacrificed, Peter said he should pity himself. Jesus turned to him and said, 'Away with you Satan, you are a stumbling block to me.' To him the devil was not a person in a red suit with horns, hooves and a toasting fork. He was someone who could speak through one of his closest friends. The words 'pity yourself' had a familiar ring. With these two words the tempter had wrought havoc in the human race.

The Last Enemy

When people hurt the Son of Man, he refused to become resentful and wallow in self pity — he just forgave them. 'Father, forgive them; for they don't know what they are doing!' Even when they were nailing him to two pieces of wood, he kept on saying it.

Nowhere is the humanity of Jesus more evident than when he was pinned to that tree. Instead of calling for a squadron of angels to free him, we hear him cry as one abandoned. 'My God, my God, why have you forsaken me?' For the first time in his life he was experiencing sin and sickness (ours not his) in his body. What was even more horrific to him was that his relationship with his Father was broken by it. What a mystery...

'It is Finished!'

Only hours before the cross, the horror of drinking our 'cup' had so gripped him that his sweat was like great drops of blood. We will never know the revulsion of the sinless one becoming sinful, the healthy body being made sick. So strong was it that he asked not to have to drink it. In the end he totally surrendered to his Father's will, and drank our cup as though it were a toast! Toward the end of his ordeal on that Roman cross-piece he drank some wine (which he had refused earlier) and shouted 'It is finished'! There was a note of triumph in his voice. His mission was accomplished. God and man were reconciled.

The veil of the temple was torn from the top to the bottom. In that dramatic gesture, God removed the unnatural division between the sacred and the secular. It was not just that he was letting man in, but that he himself was refusing to be confined. You cannot put God in a box, no matter how ornate you make it.

Seeming Defeat

The Roman officer had seen many crucifixions. Yet this one was unique. He had seen him refuse pain-killers, show concern for his mother, forgive his enemies. But it was not until Jesus' last words 'Father into your hands I commit my spirit' that the penny dropped. 'Truly, this was the Son of God,' Even death could not throw its shroud over the majesty of this man.

Yet it all had the appearance of defeat. After all he was dead. Those who had followed him were scattered. His lifeless form was lying in a rich man's tomb. The man's enemies had sealed it with an unusually heavy stone. The Romans had supplied an armed guard to make sure no one tampered with it. Behind the scenes, satanic beings, who had masterminded the whole thing, had mustered all their forces around that grave. Jesus must stay dead at all costs.

Ultimate Triumph

Just when victory seemed in their grasp, the Son of Man returned from 'that undiscovered country from whose bourne no traveller returns'. All the resources of fallen man and angels focused on that tomb were powerless to stop him. Rising from the dead, he made a public display of the weakness of the opposition. Now the victory was complete. He had conquered our last enemy — death.

The resurrection is without parallel in history. History is not only transformed by it, but must now be evaluated in the light of this epoch-making event. For the Father not only raised Christ from the dead — he also placed him on the throne of the universe (body and all), decreeing that at the name of Jesus every knee shall bow and every tongue confess that 'Jesus Christ is Lord!'

For further information read Matthew, Mark, Luke and John.

Author's Footnote

This was written 20 years ago and bears the marks and scars of my fundamentalist upbringing. To see the change in my thinking, just carry on to the next page.

APPENDIX 3

ANOTHER GNOSTIC GOSPEL

(Discovered in an old clay pot marked G.T.
somewhere around the end of the twentieth century)

'All the world's a stage' said William Shakespeare. The world stage on which we all perform is incredibly beautiful when viewed from space. As we look back at this blue planet swathed in white clouds, set against the deep darkness of space, we also realise how tiny it is. Like every other stage it gives the impression of being something it's not - solid.

When man first started to examine his surroundings, he felt the earth was built on solid building blocks. The Greeks called these blocks 'atoms', which means indestructible. At the beginning of this century man went backstage and split the atom. Solid atoms were shown to be nearly all energy. Inflate a tiny atom to the size of an Olympic stadium and its nucleus would be the size of a pea. All the rest would be energy. Now the stage was revealed for what it was - an illusion. The night sky also gives the impression of being packed with stars. But the vast majority of it would be 'empty' space with the odd star thrown in. The nearest of these stars is four light-years away. It could have stopped shining three years ago and we would be none the wiser. Looking at the night sky is like catching a glimpse of history.

Shakespeare's message is that 'all men and women are merely players'. All of us are acting all day long. Carl Jung describes the face we present to the world as our 'persona', a word used of the mask worn by classical actors. Playing our part in the globe theatre can force us to identify too much with the character we project. When the person becomes the persona, we lose sight of who we are.

Modern actors dress up and use their own face as a mask. Daily living forces us to dress for work and play our part in the scheme of things. Even those who have no job, have their 'role' in the family. Costume drama is seen at its best at weddings. Dressing up for the occasion, we announce to the world we are changing roles. Catching yourself role-playing can be the beginning of self discovery and the end of being merely a player.

'They have their exits and their entrances' said the bard. Birth and death are the only two certainties in the drama of Ordinary People. Both are traumatic. Giving birth is one of the most painful things a woman can experience. Being born is just as traumatising, but we choose to forget it. Coming naked into the world makes us feel vulnerable, so we collect things to cloak our insecurity. Because they are made of insubstantial atoms, they vanish when we leave the stage. Although we live as part of a theatrical company, we exit alone. The occasional person who manages to make it back to the theatre from the outside world, speaks of encountering a Being of light. He knew all about their lives, but never condemned them. Our mistakes, he said were part of the learning process. Learning seems to be our raison d'être - especially learning to love. But, as this tantalising glimpse cannot be 'proved', we reject the idea of life after life.

How did the world become our stage? Apparently the Owner and the Director fell out. The Owner said the staging was unreliable, and the stunts would cause a lot of pain. After an almighty row, the Director locked the Owner out of his theatre and claimed squatters rights. In his rage the Director tore up the script. He now relies on method acting. All we have to do is respond 'in character' to various life situations.

Backstage his Ariel-like crew change the scenery, issue the costumes and produce the special effects that give the illusion of reality. In reality all the cast are related to the Owner, so the theatre and all that surrounds it belongs to them. To keep the actors from discovering their true identity, the tyrannical Director forces them to perform for a living. Believing his web of lies, the rich live in poverty.

Once a carpenter unearthed the Truth. He began using it to set people free from their legally binding contracts. The Director was so furious, he decided to nail him. Using the crowd scene from Julius Caesar, he got them so worked up they killed the carpenter by mistake. But some say accounts of his death are greatly exaggerated as he was seen after the play had finished. In time, the cast, who treated the Director like some kind of god, began to lose faith in him. Some doubted there was anyone out there in the darkened theatre. Others said he was dead. Having exhausted the potential of these characters they were playing, the actors become bored. Looking for a way out, some remembered something the carpenter said. 'The Truth will set you free.' So they started to search for themselves.

Truth proved elusive until they began to pool their ideas. Then knowledge just seemed to explode. No one noticed the rebellion at first, it was so ordinary. But when the message spread to the whole cast, they stood up as one Man and confronted the Director. Exposed as a fraud, the old man fled. Chasing him and his loyal hands out of the theatre, they stumbled into the sunlight. Stunned by the beauty of the real world, they gave up the chase. Surprised at the joy of being themselves, they quit the stage. Their greatest thrill was in the discovery that they were related to the Owner. Secretly they had always admired him. Now they found they had his genes and their potential was unlimited. Being rich didn't seem to be important any more. The rapture of being alive put everything else in the shade.